OPEN HEART—OPEN HOME

OPEN HEART
OPEN HOME

KAREN BURTON MAINS

David C. Cook Publishing Co.
ELGIN, ILLINOIS—WESTON, ONTARIO
LA HABRA, CALIFORNIA

To my open-hearted parents,
Wilfred LaRue and Wilma Wicklund Burton,
who taught me about
opening doors
to soul and home.

Acknowledgments
Grateful acknowledgment is made to the following
for permission to reprint copyrighted material:

Penguin Books, Ltd: from *The Prince and Curdie,*
by George MacDonald, Puffin edition.

Macmillan Publishing Co., Inc.: from *Mere
Christianity,* by C. S. Lewis, Copyright © 1943,
1945, 1952.

Word Books; from *Full Circle,* by David Mains,
Copyright © 1971.

InterVarsity Press: from *The Church at the End of
the 20th Century,* by Francis Schaeffer, Copyright ©
1970 by L'Abri Fellowship.

"The Finest House in Town" was printed in its original
form in *Eternity* magazine, February 1974, and
is used here by permission.

FOREWORD

I commend *Open Heart–Open Home* to you, whether you are male or female, young or old, married or single.

I had only read one page when I felt a sense of excitement, and I knew this was a book I could be enthusiastic about. Karen has the gift of using words cleverly, clearly and well. Her writing is a delight to read.

But even more significant for me was the subject she chose to explore. *Hospitality because of Christ* is an almost forgotten doctrine of the faith, and yet one so desperately needed in our lonely, love-starved world.

As Karen laid the Biblical basis for this kind of open-hearted living, and shared her personal and family experiences in such a winsome way, I felt chords of agreement resonating deep within me. Hospitality is a subject close to my heart—one I consider so vital I had thought of writing something on the theme myself one day. Now I don't have to. It has been written—and I take great joy in the result.

I am eager to commend this book to you because it might very well change the way you live. It has that potential. For instance, you may find as you read that your attitudes are being challenged . . . even altered. Or you—as I—may find yourself issuing invitations you had no intention of giving even yesterday. I have just called my neighbors, some of whom have never crossed our threshold, and asked them for lunch so that together we may "celebrate the coming of spring," something I've meant to do for months (having my neighbors in, that is), but kept putting off until the "schedule loosened up a bit."

But, even if hospitality is not your gift, if having people in your home is truly not your thing, I still feel these pages hold something of value for you. I predict that as you close this book you will have been stimulated to a new quality of love, openness and sharing with the others in your life. That is exciting. For if all of us who are called by His name could respond in this way, the ministry of love unleashed in our homes, our churches, our world—would be revolutionary indeed!

Washington, D. C.   COLLEEN TOWNSEND EVANS

Contents

1

"Company's Comin' "

"COMPANY'S COMIN'!" WAS ONE OF THE JOYFUL LITANIES
our children sang when they were small. "Company's comin'!" they would intone, timing the chant to their bounces on
the living room sofa. *Company's coming!* echoed my own
child-heart. *Company's here!*

Through the years of our marriage, company has certainly
come. We have literally opened our small apartments and now
our home to hundreds and hundreds of people. Some have
come by way of invitation to formal sit-down dinners, to pancake breakfasts, or to come-home-and-help-us-clean-out-the-
refrigerator affairs. Some have come to participate in brain-
expanding idea sessions. Others have "just dropped by" to
say "Hi!" or maybe to hide awhile beneath the shelter of our
eaves. Others have come to live, to share on a daily basis the
warm circle of our family community.

Circle Church in Chicago, where my husband is a pastor,
has no building, but uses rented facilities which are available
only on Sunday mornings. So the homes of the congregation
have of necessity become central places of ministry. We meet,
eat, pray, and play in them. After receiving notice that our
lovely but aged apartment building, located in the historic Old
Town section of the city, was scheduled to be razed, my husband and I deliberately searched for a home that would ac-
commodate the most people at one time.

11

Our choice has often been validated as we observe the five-ring action that takes place in it simultaneously: worship-service planning in the living room; brainstorming sessions around the old oak dining table and the crooked, knife-scarred kitchen tables; private counseling behind the closed door of the downstairs study; a shivering prayer cell on the unheated front porch at the barest whiff of spring. It is a modest home, but it has served the Kingdom well.

Nothing is lovelier to me than filling our lives with people we love: with our children and families, with neighbors, with Christian friends. Upon making new acquaintances my first instinct is to bring them home: to flood our home and lives with humanity—its voices, its forms, its ideas, its beauty, its brokenness.

"Now, Sweet, be careful," my father used to warn. "You don't want to break your health." Hollow words, since I have come to discover that he himself was so much the source of this inexplicable inward code—this strict openness of heart and home to all people. Wasn't it he who literally raised me on the tale of the circuit-riding preacher? This story illustrated my father's standard of courtesy, or hospitality in practice. We entered no one's home without a reiteration. We were to eat all that was offered. We were not to make comments about food we didn't like. We were to remember the traveling minister who stopped for a drink of water.

While riding in the hill country, this man reined in his horse before a ramshackle cottage nestling against the back of a mountain. A little old woman finally responded to his "halloo" and was overwhelmed by her prestigious visitor. Refusing to allow him to draw his own water from the well, she made a great fuss about doing it for him.

When he took the tin cup from her hand and lifted it to draw a long draught, he realized a tiny toad was swimming in the dregs (this animal often grew from tadpole to frog depending on my father's evaluation of the needed emphasis). Rather

12

than embarrass his hostess, this gallant gentleman gulped the contents *complete*, gave thanks, and continued on his way.

With adult's eyes I admit the tale is a bit farfetched (I have since notified this particular parent of my evaluation), but as a child I was so impressed with this strict code of courtesy that if a similar opportunity had afforded itself, I, too, would have swallowed the toad!

I am a firm believer in an almost mystical transmission of values between the generations. Human beings are more than environment and genes. We are spirit, and, when sensitively nurtured, the inclination of that spirit is heightened to receive the good heritage of the spiritual world, past and present. I am persuaded that "we are surrounded by so great a cloud of witnesses." Time and finitude, those human dimensions, have nothing to do with the spiritual world where past, present and future—"the yesterday and today and for ever"—are all the same. In meditative prayer, in ministry, in hospitality, I have a sense of the weight of those others, the communion of that saintly fellowship.

At grandpa's funeral I stood in the cold March wind which whipped the loam-field smell across the tiny cemetery of my ancestors, and I knew intuitively that they were the source of this inherent need to be hospitable. "Meals were always a sacred time for us," reminisced my great-aunt Cordelia, the last survivor of the Burton clan now that my grandfather, William Mack Burton, lay beneath the rich Iowa soil. So mealtime has instinctively been for me, a sacred time. We share more than food around this table. We share life and being. It is more than a common incident in the momentum of days; it is a communion which transcends the common.

Years ago my great-grandmother Cornelia came down from the Kentucky hills at the age of 16. She married a much older widower whom she addressed as "Mr. Burton" all her life. Bearing him 11 children, she buried five in their childhood years. Devoutly religious, she was deathly ashamed of the clay

13

pipe she smoked, hiding it when visitors came to call. Her daughters called her "Mama," a gentle address for a gentlewoman.

Great-grandfather Green Barry Burton owned one of the last stagecoach lines through Kentucky. A coach, its burnished redwood highly varnished, is still stored in an obscure garage of some shirttail relation in the Blue Ridge Mountains. Yellowed photographs inadequately picture this patriarch and matriarch in their later years as handsome white-haired people. With the advent of the railroad, stagecoaching soon became extinct, and the family migrated en masse from the hill country to Illinois prairie, to Oklahoma red clay, and to Iowa corn loam. Surrealistic visions of these caravans haunt me—reminding me of Abraham wandering from Ur of the Chaldees with his nomad servants, flocks and possessions dwindling in the distance behind him. Great-grandmother Cornelia eventually became a tenant farmer's wife; but her ramrod carriage, aquiline nose, and waves of prematurely snowy hair wrapped in a high bun, bespeak simple innate aristocracy.

Looking at the pictures now stored in a dusty box, I can imagine the softly slurred hill vernacular. Imagine? No, I have heard it in her sons and daughters—great-aunts, great-uncles, and my grandfather—as they argued politics and religion and endlessly retold delightful tales about each other. I have heard it in her grandchild, my father, as he slipped from his clipped professorial urbanity to the easy backland slur of his past.

My grandfather and the other surviving five children were a tightly knit and fiercely loyal clan who upheld certain codes I never heard delineated. But even as a child I was convinced of their existence. The "shalls and shall-nots" were never verbalized to me, but their demonstrations were a surety.

Those six children grew and married, my grandfather to the daughter of a circuit-riding preacher. Tragedy hounded each generation in turn. Two of Cornelia's daughters-in-law died: my grandmother Rosa at age 26, during her third pregnancy;

the other in a flash flood. The clan rallied and took a hand in the raising of the six motherless children. Suffering left none of the progeny untouched. There were broken marriages, embittered personalities, unhappiness. There were more untimely deaths. Yet, the spirit of that clan when congregated was unique. Together, they mirrored the best of their forebears.

To this day I define "family" in terms of what I observed of that Burton clan. They exercised a high-flown hilarity with sacred Christian devotion, and combined earth-rich wisdom with antic pranks. By no means perfect people, they established loyalty as a bond and placed a high priority on compassion.

The family ritual of storytelling was remarkable. To a child like myself it was firsthand history-reporting as well as poignant homilies on the condition of mankind. Civil War tales abounded. Green Barry Burton was remarked to have fought on both sides. No turncoat he, his mare happened to wander across the lines; and the animal being more essential than the cause, my great-grandfather was forced to go Union in order to regain his rightful ownership.

The tale-weaving stretched to relatives and friends, half-brothers and sisters I have never known. Marvelous names emerge in my memory, their accompanying stories sadly forgotten. There was an Aunt Pink Hill and a renegade, "Hook" Burton, the mention of whom usually aroused comments about hanging. The foibles of these people were roundly approved, their idiosyncrasies valued. These family mythologies dance in my subconscious, weaving endless delight in humanity, capturing the passions and despairs of life into nuggets worth relating and contemplating.

Only by looking back through the dance can I comprehend my present. Whence this almost inordinate loyalty to my family? The source was certainly the comradeship I saw demonstrated in that clan. Whence this ridiculous sentimentality about children? The four of our own are a handful to raise straight in this crooked world—but, oh, how lovely to feast on little faces, to love the touch, the sound, the smell of warm, wiggling bodies.

Whence this subtle emphasis on hospitality? Certainly it is influenced by the past. The food on the long tables was a remnant of southern and southwestern tradition—Uncle Dewey's country fried chicken, hot bacon grease and vinegar dressing spilled across the greens, Aunt Bertha's special potato salad. Cold cornbread crumbled into milk, steamed bread, "the mess"—molasses poured over butter or peanut butter and stirred until it resembled creamy caramel, served up with pancakes or bread.

Food on family occasions was more than an art, more than a demonstration of gourmandism. It was a sharing, a communal expression. There was not much emphasis on elegance or finery, but a high priority on how hot the verbal debates could wax, how riotous the laughter would rage, how deeply the discussions would range. Communal sharing was symbolized by this feeding of one another. Life was celebrated in the rich enjoyment of one another's company, by the mind-stretching dissent, by the endless parading of family folklore. Those people and their times together are enhanced by a vivid memory of my grandpa fiddling country rhythms, tapping and bouncing his spry frame to encourage some fat toddler to take to dance.

These festivals dwindled as younger generations moved on, moved out. The hub of the wheel from which the spokes radiated has disintegrated. Those six children born of that thin, beautiful woman and her philosopher husband are almost gone. Mysteriously, they live on in me—a child least known to them due to distance and time. It is a demanding, yet welcome haunting. The impressions and way of life they transmitted to me are more actual than the wooden bowls and the iron pot of my grandmother's which now hang in my kitchen. These people are the source, the wellspring from which I drew long

16

unconscious draughts. They were the atmosphere I breathed. From them I inherited an innate mystique about hospitality.

Life Response

Real-life examples are extremely important as models for growth in our own lives. Read these few thought questions before continuing with the book.

1. What people do I know who display a special quality of "open heart/open home"?

2. What do these people do or say which conveys this openness?

3. Why is the hospitality of these people of importance to me? What quality in myself makes me respond to them in this certain way?

2

On Entertaining

WITH THIS WEALTH OF BACKGROUND, opening my door and issuing welcome may come easier for me than it does for others. Yet, I have discovered that even an innate inclination to hospitality must be honed and refined, embued and filled, if it is to be more than concern about centerpieces, menus, table settings and spotless rooms. For Christians, hospitality is a marvelous gift of the Holy Spirit given so that we may minister to this dying society. If our hospitality is to minister, to impart to each who crosses our threshold something of the presence of Christ—if it is to transcend the human and deal in the supernatural—there must be an agony of growth, a learning, a tutoring at the hand of the Holy Spirit.

For some, like myself, hospitality is as natural as breathing. For others, the practice must be acquired. For all, the gift must be nurtured. From this instinctive human ability, nurtured in the greenhouse of my family, the Lord has developed a spiritual aptitude in me. My hospitality, which participates in ministry, becomes a catalyst for the miraculous.

Important lessons have been learned through these years of continual open house. The first began in our honeymoon apartment when two friends stopped by, unannounced.

"You mean you spent the evening on the front porch and didn't invite them inside!" my mother exclaimed in dismay. "Karen! Haven't you heard your father insist I must never put my pride before my hospitality?"

19

Memories of my family home linger in the child part of my mind—comfortable clutter, the dining room table a collection center for books and mail and jackets, the rooms decorated with children's toys. Visitors never seemed offended, but visibly relaxed in the face of all this informality. Ties were loosened, jackets removed, shoes discarded, and feet propped up on the coffee table. My childhood pastor was one visitor who symbolized all who crossed our doorway. He invariably fell asleep on the second-hand mohair sofa murmuring, "This is the only place I can get away to relax . . ."

True hospitality comes before pride. Mother and Dad knew it had nothing to do with impressing people, but everything to do with making them feel welcome and wanted.

This primary lesson was hard-won for me. Because so many of our church activities are conducted in our homes, for many years it seemed as though I did nothing but clean up after people. One group would leave. I would vacuum. Another group would come and go. I would straighten. Another would eat. I would wash dishes.

Since I am not a housekeeper by nature, it was only natural that my inclination against such work would dominate me on occasion. One morning I picked up a neglected book and began to pursue the world between its pages with delight. By mid-afternoon, couch cushions were tilted crazily, surrounded by my son's armada of miniature cars. Newspapers tiled the carpet helter skelter, and dishes stood from last night's supper, mixed with the remains of the day's cereal and peanut butter. Then the doorbell rang. It was someone from the church.

Hospitality before pride . . . I reminded myself dismally. Determined, I welcomed the woman with warmth, invited her into the unsightly rooms and refused to embarrass her with apologies. I consciously let go of my pride and was rewarded with her amazing words, "I used to think you were perfect, but now I think we can be friends!"

From that point I began to apply the precepts learned in my

parents' home and, just in time, for I had been well on my way to becoming so involved in taking care of things that I would have found no time to be a caretaker of people.

Today I put away my pride when I open my front door and accept those standing there as they are. Consequently, I expect them to accept me as they find me. No compunctions remain about asking for help with the vacuuming, sending a seminarian upstairs to bathe a baby, giving a pile of potatoes to someone to peel. Visitors may be more than guests in our home. If they like, they may be friends.

Now when we organize a planned evening of dinner and fellowship, my husband asks guests to contribute to the meal. One brings a salad, one a dessert, one an appetizer. It is not important for me to do everything in order for the occasion to be a success. I have four children to raise, a God to know, words to share, wounds to heal. Because I've put away my pride, lovely things occur. People discover they can be hospitable to me. *Yes, we can be friends.*

One morning this week I woke and discovered that an overnight guest (who slept on the floor—all beds and mattresses being full) had filled the house with the odor of ham-and-cheese omelets cooking in the kitchen. He discovered the leak under the sink and used the morning to repair it, then stewed the ham-bone with kidney beans and served them with homemade tortillas. How far we've come. Years ago it would have been impossible for me to have offered a floor for the night—or stepped aside to be served.

Essential to hospitality is the open heart which results in an open house. These two elements are potential in every Christian, male or female, married or single. Each has a heart the Spirit is seeking to move with the things that move the heart of God. Each of us has a home—be it a small room, a modest apartment, or a mansion—in which we can practice hospitality.

For ten years my husband and I have lived in Chicago's

inner city or close to it. We have immersed our lives in the needs and problems of its inhabitants. Ours is a fractured society much in need of healing. Yet you don't have to live in the city to come to this conclusion. You need only to pick up the daily newspaper to become aware of the fragmented nature of the world.

The facts have been adequately documented. Prisons do not rehabilitate. Insane asylums are overcrowded and understaffed. The aged and the infant are abandoned. The judicial system is overworked. Social workers struggle with the frustrations of bureaucracy, too much paperwork, too-heavy caseloads. Not only are the institutions of society approaching immobilization, but a mad, erratic disorder rises frequently on the private level: children are held hostage at gunpoint, bombs are sent in the mail, parents are murdered by offspring.

This is obviously a world in which human solutions are inadequate.

The answers for the problems are found in Jesus Christ, who at the advent of His ministry announced:

> The Spirit of the Lord is upon me, because he has anointed me to preach good news to the poor. He has sent me to proclaim release to the captives and recovering of sight to the blind, to set at liberty those who are oppressed to proclaim the acceptable year of the Lord.
>
> *Luke 4:18, 19, RSV*

Christ's ministry to this impoverished, captive, blinded and oppressed world must, in one way or another, also be ours. Many of us have been given a most remarkable tool through which to minister—the miracle of a Christian home.

I am firmly convinced that if Christians would open their homes and practice hospitality as defined in Scripture, we could significantly alter the fabric of society. We could play a major role in its spiritual, moral and emotional redemption.

For the Christian, hospitality is not an option. It is an injunction. We are commended to hospitality from the example of the patriarch Abraham, who lifted a tent flap and saw three holy visitors coming to him across the burning sands, all the way to the wise counsel of the Apostle Paul.

The Levitical law declares:

> And when you reap the harvest of your land, you shall not reap your field to its very border, nor shall you gather the gleanings after your harvest; you shall leave them for the poor and for the stranger: I am the Lord your God.
>
> *Leviticus 23:22, RSV*

The prophets join in the commendation. Isaiah records these remarkable words:

> No, the kind of fast I want is that you stop oppressing those who work for you and treat them fairly and give them what they earn. I want you to share your food with the hungry and bring right into your own homes those who are helpless, poor and destitute. Clothe those who are cold and don't hide from relatives who need your help. If you do these things, God will shed his own glorious light upon you. He will heal you; your godliness will lead you forward, and goodness will be a shield before you, and the glory of the Lord will protect you from behind. Then, when you call, the Lord will answer. "Yes, I am here," he will quickly reply.
>
> *Isaiah 58:6-9, The Living Bible*

Christ's words on this subject are recorded in the Gospels:

> When you give a dinner or a banquet, do not invite your friends or your brothers or your kinsmen or rich neighbors, lest they also invite you in return, and you be repaid. But when you give a feast, invite the poor, the maimed, the lame, the blind, and you will be blessed, because they cannot repay you. You will be repaid at the resurrection of the just.   *Luke 14:12-14, RSV*

In I Timothy, Paul lists hospitality as a requirement for high office in the church, and he emphasizes in Romans that we are to "practice hospitality." I Peter 4:9 stresses this again, saying we are to "practice hospitality *ungrudgingly* to one another." The King James Version translates I Timothy 3:2:

A bishop then must be blameless, the husband of one wife, vigilant, sober, of good behaviour, *given to hospitality* . . .

Hospitality is more than just a human talent, it is a gift of the Holy Spirit. It is a supernatural ministry which, when combined with righteous living, bathed in prayer, and dedicated to the Lord, can be used by God far beyond anything we ask or think.

Scripture indicates that the Judeo-Christian heritage is rooted in hospitality. A theme of hospitality runs through the Book—a design for open-heartedness to all people. We are to share what we have with those in need. We are to open ourselves and our homes.

I am overwhelmed when I envision the results of a corporate return to the principles of Scriptural openness. For instance: Think of the impact the church could make in society if only four or five families in each congregation would care for needy children, nurturing them in love and pointing them to Christ. If a large urban area has a hundred churches, four or five homes times a hundred would involve at least four or five hundred children.

It is important that we do not think of hospitality as strictly a woman's prerogative. In fact, this ministry is also the responsibility of men—indeed, of the entire Christian family.

For most Christians, however, taking in anyone in need, even one's own family, is a radical step. Many who say they follow Christ have no comprehension of the basics of hospitality. We have allowed the world to force us into its mold. We

24

think in terms of entertaining as a woman's chance to demonstrate her skill and the quality of her home. *Entertaining has little to do with real hospitality*.

Secular entertaining is a terrible bondage. Its source is human pride. Demanding perfection, fostering the urge to impress, it is a rigorous taskmaster which enslaves. In contrast, Scriptural hospitality is a freedom which liberates.

Entertaining says, "I want to impress you with my beautiful home, my clever decorating, my gourmet cooking." Hospitality, however, seeks to minister. It says, "This home is not mine. It is truly a gift from my Master. I am His servant and I use it as He desires." Hospitality does not try to impress, but to *serve*.

Entertaining always puts things before people. "As soon as I get the house finished, the living room decorated, my place settings complete, my housecleaning done—then I will start having people in." "The So-and-so's are coming. I must buy that new such-and-such before they come." Hospitality, however, puts people before things. "We have no furniture; we'll eat on the floor." "The decorating may never get done. Please come just the same." "The house is a mess—but these people are friends. We never get to see them. Let's have this time together anyway."

Because we are afraid to allow people to see us as we really are, we welcome the false ideal of entertaining. To perpetuate the illusion we must pretend we love house cleaning, that we never put our hair in rollers, that our children are so well disciplined that they always pick up their toys. We must hint broadly that we manage our busy lives without difficulty. Working hard to keep people from recognizing our weak points, we also prevent them from loving us in our weakness.

Because hospitality has put away its pride, it doesn't care if other people see our humanness. Because we are maintaining no false pretensions, people relax and feel that perhaps we can be friends.

25

Entertaining subtly declares, "This is mine—these rooms, these adornments. This is an expression of my personality. It is an extension of who and what I am. Look, please, and admire." Hospitality whispers, "What is mine is yours." This is the secret of community that is all but lost to the church of the 20th century. "And all who believed were together and had all things in common" *Acts 2:44, RSV.* The hospitality of that first-century church clearly said, "What is mine is yours."

Entertaining looks for a payment—the words, "My, isn't she a remarkable hostess"; a return dinner invitation, a job advancement for self or spouse; esteem in the eyes of friends and neighbors. Hospitality does everything with no thought of reward, but takes pleasure in the joy of giving, doing, loving, serving.

The model for entertaining is found in the slick pages of women's magazines with their appealing pictures of foods and rooms. The model for hospitality is found in the Word of God.

In 14 years of an open house, I have never felt that people have abused the privilege. In fact, they have shown extreme concern not to take advantage. Many hands make light the work. The blessings from the practice of the gift have been overwhelming—"good measure, pressed down, shaken together, running over."

Hospitality, like charity, must begin at home. How sad it is that so many of us don't feel comfortable in our own homes. Men are not warmly welcomed at the end of a long day's hard work. Roommates live in a tense atmosphere. Children are greeted with scoldings and reprimands. Wives and husbands wait to dump frustrations on each other. How we all long to hear, "It's so good to have you home," or those other words, "It's so good to come home to you." If those dwellings we inhabit are not filled with the gentle considerations, the cherishing, the openness which earmark hospitality, it will be most difficult to extend the gift beyond our front doors.

After an attitude of openness has been developed toward our

26

immediate families, we can then more readily impart it toward those brothers and sisters in Christ, the household of faith. This marvelous refuge of acceptance and mutual support is graphically described in Ephesians 2: 19-22, RSV:

> So then you are no longer strangers and sojourners, but you are fellow citizens with the saints and members of the household of God, built upon the foundation of the apostles and prophets, Christ Jesus himself being the cornerstone, in whom the whole structure is joined together and grows into a holy temple in the Lord; in whom you also are built into it for a dwelling place of God in the Spirit.

When have we experienced such unity? Our churches are filled with strangers and sojourners. The homes and lives of our congregations are often closed to one another. Efforts at *entertaining*, with the emphasis on things and pride, often build more gaps than they bridge. How much today's church needs to be bathed in unselfish, loving, accepting hospitality.

Unless we develop a true spirit of acceptance in our church families, the hospitality we extend to our world will be hypocritical. When our immediate homes and the household of God are what our Lord intended them to be, we will naturally extend an attitude of openness to our neighbors around us. It is appalling how few Christians have entered into the lives of their immediate neighborhoods. These are a nearby inheritance to which our Father desires us to minister. How few of us are trying to find ways to serve our neighbors, to extend mercy. Often our official Christianity—our meetings and commitments—make us less accessible to them rather than more available.

Once the gift of hospitality has been developed in our homes, churches, and neighborhoods, we can begin to participate in a larger and more difficult effort: that of playing roles of significance in our society.

This ministry to society cannot be accomplished without the utter abandonment of ourselves to God. He will fill us with His Spirit and allow us to participate in healing and redemptive works completely unfathomable to us, if we are open to Him.

What a sin it is that many Christians know so little about this broken world. They have isolated themselves from the starvation of nations, turned their backs on battered and abandoned babies. Little do they care that children grow without a gentle touch, that old men haunt park benches dying from loneliness rather than age. This world to many believers is one large, silent scream. We refuse to hear the agony—of children too hungry to cry, of mothers with breasts gone dry, without energy to moan, of impoverished peoples numbed with outrage, of Indian youths suicided by despair.

O God, help us to hear, to hear those cries without fear for ourselves, and with compassion for those who mourn. Help us to listen to those in need, without thought for our own material treasures. Help us to seek to be like Christ, upon whom was the Spirit of the Lord.

If Christians, corporately, would begin to practice hospitality, we could play significant roles in redeeming our society. There is no better place to be about the redemption of society than in the Christian servant's home; and the more we deal with the captive, the blind, the downtrodden, the more we realize that in this inhospitable world, a Christian home is a miracle to be shared.

In Webster's dictionary, the definition for hospitable is wedged between the word "hospice," which is a shelter, and the word "hospital" which is a place of healing. Ultimately, this is what we offer when we open our home in the true spirit of hospitality. We offer shelter; we offer healing.

When we give, having put away our pride, then Christ sanctifies the simple gift. He makes it holy, useful. My three-dollar oak table has become an altar where hungry hearts have been nourished with the Bread of Life, where thirsty spirits have received the Living Water. Our living room has been made a sanctuary where sacraments of comfort and communion have been offered, where we have shared in the fellowship of human suffering and human delight. More perfect to me than the praise, "You entertain beautifully!" is the whisper of the young girl who had just come to know Christ, "Thank you for having me. God is here in this home."

This really is the essence of hospitality, a heart open to God, with room prepared for the Guestness of the Holy Spirit, which welcomes the Presence of Christ. This is what we share with those to whom we open our doors. We give to them Him and think nothing of what we give of ourselves.

Perhaps your children sing, "Company's comin'!" or maybe you have a guest night scheduled on your calendar. Perhaps your doorbell is ringing. May I ask you my father's question? Where is your hospitality? Where is your pride?

Life Response

Equipment needed: Pencil or pen, paper, and about 15 minutes of time.

1. What excuses do you find yourself giving as reasons for not practicing hospitality? List them.

2. Consider which of these stem from pride and mark them with a "P."

3. Make a resolve to practice this good discipline: The next time someone drops by unexpectedly, promise yourself you will attempt to extend a warm welcome. This means that even if you have to soon excuse yourself to rush off to an appointment, you will make the drop-in feel welcome. Remember, good friends are hard to find.

3

The Imminent Guest

GEORGE MACDONALD, THE SCOTTISH MINISTER who lived during the early 19th century, has written the marvelous children's fantasies, *The Princess and the Goblin* and *The Princess and Curdie*. Perhaps one reason I like these books is because God is symbolized by the figure of the wise and mysterious great-great-grandmother Irene. In the second book there is a section of which I am particularly fond. Curdie, the miner's son, has been sent from the mountains to undertake a treacherous assignment. Before he leaves he is commissioned by Irene.

Up into her tower he climbs, winding through the multiple passages, then into her remarkable chamber. Curiously he notices that on the hearth a fire is glowing. It is a fire of roses which burn and give forth a sweet pungency, yet they are not consumed. "Curdie," says the great-great-grandmother, who now appears in a form of youth and beauty. "You have stood more than one trial already, and have stood them well: now I am going to put you to a harder." She instructs him to thrust his hands into the fire. He obeys, enduring the intense pain only to discover, when he is given permission to take them out, that his hands have not been destroyed or charred, but are rather as white and smooth as those of the princess.

"Now here is what the rosefire has done for you," explains the princess. "It has made your hands so knowing and wise, it has brought your real hands so near the outside of your flesh gloves, that you will henceforth be able to know at once the hand of a man who is growing into a beast . . . . According, then, to your knowledge of that beast will be your knowledge of the man you have to do with. Only there is one beautiful and awful thing about it, that if any one gifted with this perception once uses it for his own ends, it is taken from him, and then, not knowing that it is gone, he is in a far worse condition than before, for he trusts to what he has not got."

I wonder how much George MacDonald understood the Scriptural doctrine of the Holy Spirit and spiritual gifts. This short passage contains many excellent symbols relating to these Christian concepts. Our discipleship is certainly a treacherous mission on which we are sent by our Lord; but before we do His work in this world, He bids us cast ourselves into the rosyfire of Himself. In obedience we must yield to His burning, be it chastisement or agonies of spiritual warfare, or the dismays of ordinary circumstances or suffering. Here the stubby chaff and the cherished dross are destroyed, the soul-callouses are smoothed. We withdraw ourselves, refined and new, childlike again.

When we have yielded ourselves in obedience to our Lord, opened our lives to the indwelling of His Spirit, and pleaded to be purified by the fire of His Presence, we discover with delight that He has endowed us with marvelous tools to aid us in our missions. Curdie is fitted with a gift of discernment which not only saves his own life and that of the people he loves, but helps him rescue the Kingdom from the doom of evil.

We too can have similar surprising abilities. But before we discuss the manifestations of spiritual gifts we must achieve a clearer understanding of the role of the Holy Spirit.

The Holy Spirit is real and His power is available to us. He is not a discussion of words or a statement of creed. Through His infilling, we have Christ within our beings. Most of us will agree to this. Yet there is controversy over the question of "how does one *get* the Holy Spirit?" The question itself is flawed; it treats Christ through His Spirit as a commodity to be acquired or a goal to be achieved. Rather we should ask, "How do we allow the Holy Spirit to *get* us?"

Unfortunately, many of us come to this question influenced by our own experience and of the Christian brethren with whom we feel comfortable. It is as difficult to look at the Scriptural teachings on this subject with impartiality as it is to be neutral in judging the people we love—children, husband, friends, parents. Realizing that volumes have been written on this topic, I will attempt to give a simple explanation, admitting all the while my own obvious and hidden partialities, so that the role of the Spirit and His gifts can be applied to the use of hospitality in our unredeemed world.

Scripture does clearly teach that the mark of the Christian is the Spirit of Christ who dwells within each believer. Romans 8: 9 states, "But you are not in the flesh, you are in the Spirit, if in fact the Spirit of God really dwells in you. Any one who does not have the Spirit of Christ does not belong to him" (RSV). In the same chapter the author reiterates in verse 14: "For all who are led by the Spirit of God are sons of God." I John 3: 24 is another example of this truth: "All who keep his commandments abide in him, and he in them. And by this we know that he abides in us, by the Spirit which he has given us." This is the basic premise: *The Spirit dwells within each Christian.*

The history of the early church as recorded in the Book of Acts is essentially a history of the church under the leadership of the Holy Spirit. It is a chronicle of the results which the Spirit is working within the believers, and the effect on the corporate body of believers. What we now familiarly term conversion occurred almost without exception in a threefold manner: 1. A person proclaimed the name of Christ as his Savior and Lord. His mind decided, "Yes, I believe and will follow this Christ and become a part of His Kingdom." 2. He repented of his sins, entering the waters of baptism as a visual act of following Christ into death, but also to symbolize turning from error and trusting to God to wash away the sins of the past. 3. He submitted to the filling of the Holy Spirit, either through the laying on of hands or through what I call spontaneous combustion—when the Spirit naturally "fell out" on believers.

All these steps generally followed in short order, one upon another. Peter, in his powerful sermon delivered on the day of Pentecost, exhorts (after he identifies an atmosphere of belief on the part of his audience), "Repent, and be baptized every one of you in the name of Jesus Christ for the forgiveness of your sins; and you shall receive the gift of the Holy Spirit" (Acts 2: 38).

In Acts 8 the apostles in Jerusalem receive the word that Samaria has responded to Philip's message of Christ and to his demonstrations of power. The story continues with verse 14:

> Now when the apostles at Jerusalem heard that Samaria had received the word of God, they sent to them Peter and John, who came down and prayed for them that they might receive the Holy Spirit; for it had not yet fallen on any of them, *but they had only been baptized in the name of the Lord Jesus.*

This last italicized phrase indicates that something more is desired for the Spirit to fall on these people. The following verse explains what was to become a norm for the New Testament church *but never a binding pattern.* "Then they laid their hands on them and they received the Holy Spirit" (vs. 17).

Simon, the magician, is intrigued by the demonstrated authority of these apostles and the narrative records: "Now when Simon saw that the Spirit was given through the laying on of the apostles' hands, he offered them money. . . ." He was sharply rebuked and informed that the gift of the Spirit could not be bought.

The order of these three parts of conversion was often reversed, such as in the case of the conversion of the Apostle Paul. I imagine in the three days between the brilliant encounter on the road to Damascus and the knock of Ananias at the door, Saul had deeply considered the claims of his Lord—"I am Jesus whom you are persecuting." Ananias in obedience sought out this one-time inquisitor:

> And laying his hands on him he said, "Brother Saul, the Lord Jesus who appeared to you on the road by which you came, has sent me that you may regain your sight and be filled with the Holy Spirit." And immediately something like scales fell from his eyes and he regained his sight. Then he rose and was baptized, and took food and was strengthened (Acts 9: 17-19).

We can safely assume that the hands which conveyed healing also brought to Paul the filling of the Holy Spirit. He immediately went to the synagogue and began to proclaim Christ as Lord. All three ingredients of conversion are noted, but in new order.

Sometimes there is such an atmosphere of belief that the Spirit comes without the laying on of hands. Such was the case with the Gentile Cornelius, a devout man whom God used as an illustration to the Jewish church of His impartial love. (See Acts 10: 44-48.)

A study of the book of the Acts of the Apostles (some think it should be called the book of the Acts of the Holy Spirit) reveals that the infilling of the Holy Spirit was an integral part of the circumstances of conversion.

However, when I think about the preaching and practical observances of my own past, is it any wonder I grew up with such a foggy conception of the Holy Spirit? Conversion was limited pretty much to "gettin' saved," and that meant being snatched from the pit. Water baptism, despite my Baptist background, centered more on controversy—dunking versus sprinkling; and, though necessary, it was an act of obedience to a symbol which was difficult to relate to modern life. I laughed recently when a young friend explained the circumstances of his water baptism. "The pastor just said, 'We don't really understand this, but we do it anyway, because our Lord told us we should.'"

Hands were never laid upon me for the gift of the Holy Spirit. This elementary doctrine (Heb. 6: 2) was reserved only for those entering professional ministry. Moreover, I was never told that upon making my declaration of belief in Christ I could expect the Spirit to indwell me with Christ's very Presence. The whole subject of the Holy Spirit was shrouded by confusion.

The historical record of the church on this issue hasn't been consistent. Often the reception of grace was reduced to formula (the confirmation service before a child takes his first communion is directly related to the apostolic laying on of hands for the filling of the Holy Spirit of the New Testament church). And many 15th-century reformers, reacting to man-made formulas, threw out important babies with dirty bathwater in their occasional overstatement of protest. This doctrine of the Spirit, which was supposed to occur in harmony with one's verbal confession of Christ and in relation to the entering of baptismal waters, has been mired throughout the centuries in controversial muck. Fortunately, God is not limited by our ignorance and has chosen in His grace to work in His children's lives through a variety of ways.

My own home is an illustration of this. David, my husband, did experience the infilling of the Spirit at conversion. At 13 he was hungry for a deep experience of salvation. He testifies to locking himself in the bathroom with His Bible so he would not be disturbed while searching the Scriptures. One night, he finally, from the depths of his young soul, cried out to be saved, and knew assuredly that instant gratification which comes to some, that Christ had heard and answered his prayers. He was

bathed in peace—a release of guilt and an assurance. I believe
he was given the measure of the Spirit in accord with his hungry heart. That evening he was set aside unto the Lord, and,
when I first met him, the most outstanding characteristic about
David was that he was first and foremost a man of God.

Even though I became a Christian at an early age, I knew
next to nothing of the work of the Holy Spirit, even on a basic
intellectual level. Later, after we had begun Circle Church and
were examining the Scriptures, I began to grow. I could remember vague references from my past to this third Person of
the Trinity, but nothing which had changed my life. After we
discovered the work of the Spirit on the pages of His Book, I
began to look and listen for His voice and work in my life. I
think I fell into the category described by A. W. Tozer: "Every Christian has the Holy Spirit, but the Holy Spirit doesn't
have every Christian." As yet I had not discovered the need to
yield myself so totally that the Spirit could "have" me.

It wasn't until after our fourth child was born that I began to
sense the lack of depth in my discipleship. I recognized the
subtle self which hindered me from allowing the Lord to channel Himself through my life. There was obvious neglect of the
Scripture and of prayer. I then began a pursuit of God, my own
hungering after the Holy Spirit. It was a gnawing consumption.
I wanted Him and none other. One night it was as though He
called me from my bed, and I woke to do soul-business in my
husband's study. I yielded my body a living sacrifice and cried
out, flat on my face, "Lord, I give You all I am; now You give
me all You have for me!"

Though this experience was not ecstatic (I didn't speak in
tongues) or emotional (I didn't weep or laugh), it was real. I
knew beyond a shadow of a doubt I had been filled, or more
descriptively, been entirely possessed by Him.

The point of this testimony is to state that my experience in
the Spirit has been different from that of my husband's, which
more closely mirrored the New Testament sequence of con-

version. How utterly foolish it would be for each of us to refuse to accept each other's testimony and insist we duplicate the other's experience. David could deny I had been filled with the Spirit years after confessing Christ as Lord and point to Scriptures which demonstrate that the Spirit accompanies conversion. How fruitless it would be if I insisted he submit to a "second blessing" of the Spirit even though his life has obviously demonstrated godliness—hours in the Word, a love of prayer, the growth of holiness, the release of gifts such as prophecy and evangelism, and the overcoming of sin. This dialogue of tension would have ruined our marriage, and it is exactly the kind of friction which has divided the church. Instead we try to allow the Lord to work in our lives as He wills and at the point of our individual needs.

Once Christians have achieved an understanding of the Holy Spirit based on Scripture, they need to accept the fact that the Spirit works uniquely in the lives of individual believers. We must be careful to present the concept of conversion fully, including the coming of the Holy Spirit, and then work to find the methods which will most closely harmonize with New Testament patterns. We need to point one another to the Lord with the confidence that He indeed can teach each of us what it is we need. We must come to cherish our own experience, but not to the point of insisting that others duplicate it. We must delight in the unique way God calls each of us to holiness, and realize that His works among the children of men are as different from one another as the stars are from the sands of the seas. There are norms in Scripture, but even the record of the New Testament church shows how the Spirit acts differently as He sees fit!

How then do we know when we have received this gift which is the cornerstone of so much New Testament teaching? There are several ways. First there is an inward assurance due to the active presence of the Spirit within. I John 2:26 reads, ". . . but the anointing which you received from him abides in you, and you have no need that any one should teach you; as his anointing teaches you about everything, and is true, and is no lie, just as it has taught you, abide in him.'' Personal certainty is difficult to prove to the outsider, but when you have it, *you know you have it*.

Second, there will be release, instant or more gradual, of certain of the gifts of the Holy Spirit. It is true that Scripture demonstrates that the filling of the Holy Spirit was often accompanied by the gift of tongues, and I believe this occurs validly today. However, the record in Acts reveals that many other gifts of the Spirit were displayed after His coming, and these are overlooked in our heated discussions concerning the pros and cons of the gift of tongues. For example, the believers shared all things in common (true hospitality); they gave to those in need; they spoke of the Lord with boldness (Acts 2: 4, 43; 4: 31). In just these short passages we can detect not only these gifts but also a description of such examples as administration, miracles, healings, acts of mercy, prophecy, exhortation.

Some of the gifts were instantaneous, like tongues; others came gradually. Paul's teaching on gifts in I Corinthians 12 indicates that the gifts were uniquely distributed.

> Now there are varieties of gifts, but the same Spirit; and there are varieties of service, but the same Lord; and there are varieties of working, but it is the same God who inspires them all in every one (vss. 4-6).
>
> Are all apostles? Are all prophets? Are all teachers? Do all work miracles? Do all possess gifts of healing? Do all speak with tongues? Do all interpret? (vs. 29)

Accordingly, we must be careful not to insist that the manifestation of the Spirit is always centralized in the demonstration of one of the gifts—speaking in tongues. Rather we can more safely say that one test of whether we have been filled with His Spirit is whether we have experienced a release in our life of any of His gifts.

The third test of the Spirit in our lives is whether the fruits of the Spirit are developing, coming to ripeness. These fruits differ from the gifts in that they are qualities of personality which mirror integrity, while the gifts are abilities which enhance our service. The fruits of the Spirit prove our claim to the gifts of the Spirit. Without these qualities of goodness, our works are meaningless. Without love, our oration is like empty gongs clanging, our kindness is ashes, our doing hypocritical. The fruits are a measure of the validity of our service.

These then are three ways we can identify the work of the Holy Spirit in our lives. Is there an inward certainty that He is present? Are we seeing demonstrations of surprising supernatural abilities in serving others? Is an inner harmony developing, a wholeness in our persons?

It is tremendously important not to limit the filling of the Spirit to only one occasion. He is not static, but (to employ an overused term) He is existential, or of this moment. He comes again and again with His gifts and His fruits to renew our strength and to gratify our needs. When we minister to the world, He ministers to us. I have come to learn how important it is to sit in silence before my Maker. The time for words and pleas and explanations is over. The Word has been studied and now the pages are shut. Now to listen. Now to keep one's mind fixed on Him. Now to be silent. Often when I leave these times of contemplation I am filled with His Presence, and filled again and again. The more we learn the discipline of yieldedness, the more we understand the meaning of dependence, the more we experience of Him.

When seeking Him, we must refuse to allow ourselves to be caught in that emotional trap of looking for bright lights or sensations. We do not look for experience, but for Him. We do not seek blessings, but Him. We don't even hunt for the gifts, but for Him. When we have found the Spirit, then blessing, experience, and gifts are ours; but He chooses the ways and the manifestations and the times. We keep our hearts listening, content to allow Him to decide how to meet us.

How appropriate was the infilling of the Holy Spirit to my experience of hospitality. Prior to my personal meeting with Him, we had always opened our home to those we met through our work. Now He was teaching me to yield everything, my dwelling as well as my soul, to His Guestness. "Come, Lord Jesus. Be our Guest," was no longer the prattled singsong of the children at table, but the deep cry of my heart. At night, lying on the pillow, I would invite Him to inhabit our home, to fill every room with His love. In prayer I would imagine the very atmosphere being softened by His response to my invitation. There He was quietly rocking in the children's rooms as they slept, peace and gentleness surrounding their dreams.

Fill our home, Lord, with Yourself. Let us give to those who come, You. He comes, this Guest, externally in the rooms and internally in our souls. Here He is in His immanence and in His transcendence.

We must be aware when we open our lives and our homes to His Guestness, that we, like Curdie, will experience a rosyfire. The Spirit must break our practice of the presence of self, and He does this by forging Himself into our inner being. How often these last years have I been filled with that burning? There were times when I literally felt as though He grabbed my soul with His holy fist and lifted me up before His face with my feet dangling in midair and my tongue protesting "No, Lord, I can't take anymore. No more, Lord. I'm weary of the painful growth."

I am learning about those flames which burn but do not consume. I am learning about that fire which releases the odor and fragrance of roses and about that Guest who inhabits the parlor of our souls, who banks the fireplace with ashes to keep the burning low or who uses the billows when the room has grown cold.

Welcome, Lord, our most imminent Guest. We open to You the doors of all these rooms, in life or heart or home.

Life Response

Spend some time considering these personal test questions regarding the Imminent Guest:

How would you rate the role of the Holy Spirit in your life? Use A. W. Tozer's evaluation—Do you "have" the Spirit; or does the Spirit "have" you?

Is the Spirit just a "downstairs" Guest, only allowed to occupy those company rooms? Has He as yet been invited into the expensive tool shop where the equipment is rusting from lack of use? Or to those places where the beds are unmade or where sinks are filthy or closets cluttered?

Pray the prayer of invitation at the close of this chapter. Pray it daily and then learn to listen when He knocks at one of the closed doors.

4

The Gift of Hospitality

HOW CAN A CORRECT PHILOSOPHY regarding the gifts of the Holy Spirit affect one's practice of hospitality? In order to determine this we must draw some conclusions from the four Scriptural passages which essentially deal with spiritual gifts. Pertinent information is found in I Corinthians 12; Romans 12; Ephesians 4; and I Peter 4.

1. *The listing of the kinds of gifts in Scripture are illustrative.* Many scholars feel that the gifts listed in the letters to New Testament churches are exclusive, in other words, they are closed; no others can be added. In light of the fact, however, that the lists are different, and the lists of Romans, I Corinthians, and Ephesians are written by the same teacher, Paul, I prefer to view them as *illustrative,* opening up the possibility that other gifts exist besides those catalogued in these passages. For instance: Since childhood I have recognized that my writing abilities were a gift from my Heavenly Father. However, since I have matured in faith, I see the Spirit working through this ability in surprising ways, and I now regard it as a spiritual gift. There are others with musical and dramatic gifts, none of which are mentioned in the lists, but all of which can contribute in ministry to the healthy life of Christ's body.

Understanding that these Scriptures are illustrating *kinds* of gifts of the Holy Spirit, rather than giving an exclusive list, aids greatly in the use of our personal gifts. It broadens our base of discovery and enables us to begin with obvious abilities, then allow the Spirit to develop them to surprising supernatural degrees.

2. *Each Christian has at least one gift of the Holy Spirit, and most have many.* This is obvious from the Scripture. "To *each* is given the manifestation of the Spirit . . ." (I Cor. 12: 7); "All these are inspired by one and the same Spirit, who apportions to *each* one individually as he wills " (vs. 11); "As *each* has received a gift, employ it for one another " (I Pet. 4: 10). The temptation for many is to protest, "But . . . but I don't *have* any abilities." This attitude is unscriptural. It may be a true statement of our feelings, but it is one case where our intellect must overrule. We may feel unable to contribute, but we must train our intelligence to accept those verses which teach that each Christian has been given gifts to be used within the church. Then it becomes a matter of asking in prayer that our Father will assist us in discovering and using our gifts.

Most Christians have more than one gift, and as they develop their talents, proving themselves trustworthy, their Master often gives more in quantity and enables them to achieve higher quality. The familiar parable of the talents in Matthew 25 reiterates this theme. The Master goes on a long journey assigning his property to the care of three servants. To one he gives five talents (one talent is roughly equal to one thousand dollars), to one he gives two talents, to the last he gives one.

The first two stewards double their portions, while the last hides his in the ground. Upon returning, the Master is angered at this servant's lack of discretion and chides him for not at least collecting interest from a bank. He then gives the one talent to the one who has proved himself most worthy. This is the way of spiritual gifts. Entrusted with the property of our Lord, we are expected to develop it in His interests. To those who are most faithful, He often gives more.

3. *The gifts are always to be used for ministry.* "To each is given the manifestation of the Spirit *for the common good*"

(I Cor. 12: 7). "To equip the saints for the work of ministry, for building up the body of Christ" (Eph. 4: 12). "As each has received a gift, employ it for one another" (I Pet. 4: 10).

Ministry is a word that is sometimes misunderstood. Instead of relating the concept strictly to paid professionals we must come to realize that Scripture teaches that we are all ministers. We are to use our gifts to nourish fellow human beings, but particularly those within the body of Christ. Ministry is not just the work of a church staff, but something of which we all must partake, whether we bear a title or not.

4. *All of the gifts are supernatural.* Some of these abilities listed in Scripture, such as an innate human ability to work miracles or healings seem *supernatural,* while gifts such as contributing financially or giving physical aid appear to fall under the category of *natural* abilities. Yet all of the gifts are supernatural.

Some of the gifts of the Holy Spirit, it is true, spring from abilities that may have existed before we became Christians. We may have been skilled teachers in the public schools, for example. The difference between this remaining a highly crafted skill, and a gift of the Spirit infused with supernatural life is basically found in one's attitude. Our mindset should be one of yieldedness which can become habitual by the regular check of three simple questions:

1. Am I willing to use this talent in ministry?
2. Does sin in my life restrict God's being able to use this talent in ministry?
3. Do I continually tell God I am dependent on His supernatural working to transform my talent into a gift of the Holy Spirit?

A "No" answer to any of these will diminish the possibilities of our natural talents being used in a supernatural way. If we are not willing to use a talent in ministry, we cannot expect to view it as a gift, since ministry is the only purpose for which gifts exist. We must be careful, lest we have the gift taken away; and then, not knowing that it is gone, we are in a far worse condition than before, because we trust to what we have not got.

Often the professional has great difficulty using within the church those same skills which he finds so useful in the secular market. This is because we are not willing to lay aside our sense of ego, the competitive nature, the desire for credit, and to simply do our tasks as unto the Lord. When the world measures one's abilities in terms of financial remuneration, it is difficult to develop an attitude which measures worth in terms of the effect on others' lives. However, once the professional discovers the meaning of ministry within the church, he is able to apply those same principles to his job.

The largest problem facing the lay person is how to relate his Christianity to his real life. The secret to the answer is found in understanding the working of the gifts of the Holy Spirit. A close friend had yielded herself to the Holy Spirit and begun to grope with the meaning of the gifts of healing. An excellent teacher and musician, she taught music in a private inner-city school where there were many emotionally distraught children. In a small prayer cell, she voiced her concern about the children and sought wisdom as to how to minister in her profession. She had decided she wanted to use her abilities in ministry in her classroom.

Every morning she was assigned to monitor the cafeteria before school. She took her Bible and spent that half-hour in prayer, asking God to fill the troubled school with His presence. Private lessons gave her close physical contact with students. Laying her hands casually on some troubled child, she would instruct music, all the while praying that God would use her as a channel for His healing, that He would fill the disordered personality with love and restore any chemical imbalance. She chose musicals for teens to perform that would stimulate religious thinking, selections from the musical *Godspell,* and a contemporary cantata on Amos, the narration of which was taken straight from Scripture.

She began to witness surprising responses on the behalf of those problem children as well as spiritual resistance, particularly as it related to her administration. At the end of the year, wearied and a little worn from the efforts, she was rewarded by the words of the special education teacher who said that in "all of her years of teaching she had never had so much success with so many difficult cases." Little did the other teacher realize the hours of prayer, as well as the application of the gifts of teaching and music, that had aided her.

The second question to ask of our attitude toward our gifts deals with personal righteousness: Does sin in my life restrict God's being able to use this talent in ministry? Often we don't realize the effect of unrighteousness on our service. Each unconfessed sin, each cherished memory of bitterness, each resentment blocks the flow of the Spirit through us to others. My husband testifies to standing in the pulpit and being aware he was not speaking within the work of the Spirit because of some hidden matter in his heart. Empty, cardboard-tasting, devoid of God's Presence—this experience is one he does not wish to duplicate. The pulpit and the exposition of the Word of life are awesome responsibilities, and he has become careful to plead, "Create in me a clean heart, O Lord; and renew a right spirit within me."

So it is with all the gifts of the Spirit. Their effectiveness is increased in direct proportion to our holiness. The regular practices of confession and forgiveness must be applied in order to keep these gifts in utility.

The last question deals with dependency and is really a watershed. If we give no thought to needing God's intervention, we really have not grasped the difference between working out of our humanity and working in the surprising supernatural. The tricky thing about dependency is that we often do see results when we forge out in our own strength. But we soon discover that human efforts are seldom lasting, and we realize that apart from the empowering of God we can't find the words that change a couple's divorce-headed marriage into one of love; we can't sing words to an audience that will bring conviction to sin-filled hearts; we can't find power to give a homosexual the strength to change. When God works through us, we suddenly realize people are testifying to lasting changes in their lives because of our ministry. *Did I say that? Did I do that?* we find ourselves asking, and we suddenly realize that it was Him working through us.

"Am I dependent on God?" is the basic question. Am I dependent when I use my well-honed teaching skills with these Sunday school children? Do I want to give them content, or do I want them to incorporate difficult truths into their lives? Am I dependent even in giving money out of my vast resources? Am I content with routine tithing, or do I want to be sensitive to the Spirit's whisper about a certain independent missionary couple only to discover months later that they were near starving? Am I dependent to open my home in hospitality? Am I content with people chewing food and spewing words or do I want to experience that bond of heart to heart, soul to soul, mind to mind? Am I dependent, *continually,* on God's help, or am I able to do it alone?

This is the essence of I Peter 4:11: The apostle is discussing attitude changes. "Whoever speaks, as one who utters oracles of God; whoever renders service, as one who renders it by the strength which God supplies; in order that in everything God may be glorified through Jesus Christ." With which are you content? Speaking, or uttering oracles of God? Rendering service, or doing it with unwearying reservoirs of strength?

5. *All of the gifts must be developed.* Often the Lord awakens in us abilities which seem to have no relationship to our natural talents. The gifts of healing, the gifts of knowledge and of tongues, often appear to come spontaneously. These, how-

ever, need as much work as those others which are more familiar. Sometimes these can't be called forth at will, but are given precisely to meet the need of a particular person at a particular time.

My customary activity during the worship service on Sunday morning is to be in an attitude of prayer and praise. Praying for the one who is preaching, I request that the gift of prophecy or teaching will be freed, for people in the congregation to be convicted of truth, for healing of emotion or body. It is not unusual to receive a sense of someone in trouble. For a while I was content just to sit still with this knowledge, but soon I learned that the gift had been given for ministry and that my Lord expected me to do something about those he laid on my heart. Sometimes I know who needs a word of encouragement, or extra love. Other times I have to wait until that person is brought to me. The development of this gift is rooted in sensitivity to the voice of the Spirit, of learning to know when it is Him speaking to me, and of comprehending what it is I am supposed to do with the knowledge.

A surprising example of this gift occurred on a week's vacation I took with friends in Denver. Exhausted myself, I had been shipped off by my husband, with my typewriter, to find some rest and time for the writing deadlines that were looming. At the end of my week's stay, we attended a newly formed house church. I wasn't looking for ministry. Anonymity was delightful and my recent weariness prohibited the expenditure of much energy. I had spent much time, however, enjoying the company of my Lord in those mountains. We sat in the crowded family room for the worship service, and during communion I became aware that our hostess was carrying what I felt was fresh grief. Someone else was experiencing depression. During the communal prayer time, I lifted these people before the Lord and asked that the light of His love would hold them.

That little group shared such a loving sense of warm fellowship, and when we left I inquired of my friend if she knew anything about the woman the Lord had laid on my heart. "Oh, yes," she replied. "I just discovered this week they had recently lost a teenage son in a skiing accident." Since I was leaving the next morning, there was no time for additional ministry, and I felt the Lord had given me that knowledge to be able to carry some burdens in prayer, which I have done.

All the gifts must be bathed in prayer. Often while in prayer I will receive clearer understanding as to the Lord's specific purposes at work through the gifts. The first time I was aware of the gift of knowledge I had been simply enjoying the quiet of the presence of the Lord. He began to lay on my heart, very insistently, the name of a woman in our church. I went to the phone and called her, only to find she was hastening out the door on the way to the hospital for emergency treatment. I was so amazed at the timing behind this I didn't know what to say. Now I would be able to convey God's love and concern, "God loves you greatly in this time of your trouble. He has placed you in my heart with a great sense of His love and wants me to communicate this to you." We gradually learn how to use the gifts by practicing them, and if they are real, the body of believers will affirm them by reporting the value of our ministry to us.

6. *God speaks to the Church and through the Church by means of the gifts of the Holy Spirit.* Sadly, 20th-century man has great difficulty in knowing the mind of God. Western man, rationally oriented, too often worships his own mental acuity. Hounded by schedules, hurrying through an electricity-driven society, he will not slow down to hear a God who sometimes only speaks to us in silence.

The picture of the body of Christ given to us by Paul is beautiful in its unity and harmony. Each member is employing his gift specialty for the good of the others, not envious, but each in love acting as recipient of another's ministry. Each is functioning, not merely out of flawed and exhausted humanity, but directed by a supernatural Head, with co-laborers under His direction. An ideal by no means easy to achieve, it is nevertheless the picture of a mature body, lithe with muscles rippling, middle-age at its best, physical coordination combined with seasoned beauty, every inch, every cell sparked with the life of Christ.

What a rare thing for the world to see—harmony and unity! When I begin to allow the Spirit to function through my gifts, and when you begin the same process, when we soak ourselves in Scripture and saturate our hearts in prayer, when we learn what submitting one to another means, then we will have something to say not only to one another, but to this calloused and critical world. The Spirit is able to speak to the Church through the gifts of the Holy Spirit, and He is then able to speak through the Church to the world.

How then does all this apply to hospitality? We must look at hospitality as we would at any other gift. Am I willing to use my home, my sports equipment, and my table settings (or lack of them) in ministry? If so, then I must first ask the Lord to sensitize me to which people need a special touch of love and to help me determine the best form of service. Does sin in my life restrict God's being able to use this talent in ministry? Again I must come to that kneeling place and ask the Spirit to search the heart, to make me open to a washing of my soul. Do I continually tell God I am dependent on His supernatural working to transform my talent into a gift of the Holy Spirit? "Company's comin' "—*O Lord, give me love for these varied people. Help me to have an open heart as well as an open door. Let me not be concerned about how things look or how things taste to the exclusion of how people feel. Help me to give to them You.*

Often over the years people have asked, "How do you do it? People are always coming and going in your house." My neighbors particularly have noticed. They observe the swinging front door and are sometimes inconvenienced in a search

51

for a parking space. One Catholic friend reported her husband's comment, "Tom says that anyone who can have people in her home at seven o'clock every Saturday morning must be a saint!" To be perfectly honest, I must admit to some rather unsaintly feelings about that early morning staff meeting, particularly in regard to the one staff member who regularly arrived one half hour early—at six-thirty!

These comments came often enough that I began to pride myself on my excellent management. Then one day the truth hit me—I wasn't an excellent manager at all! It was the release of the Spirit within me that was enabling me to practice this gift with such ease. The gifts were in operation. I was experiencing "the strength which God supplies"! It was one of the gifts of the Holy Spirit, hospitality, which made it so easy to open the front door, again and again; to search through cupboards and discover a forgotten can tucked in a corner; to buy just the right ingredients for a certain unplanned dish; to bring home extra groceries because of a sale, and thus have food handy for those unexpected mouths.

Then I began to understand how the gifts make ministry bearable. Without them, we wear out, burn out, grind out. I thought of all those dear pastors, of exhausted missionaries, worn beyond words, broken in spirit, who had not fully enjoyed the infilling, liberating gift of the Spirit and His consequent grace to continue the hard work of giving. Martin Luther knew the meaning of this concept when he penned those words to "A Mighty Fortress Is Our God," that great hymn of spiritual warfare. "The Spirit and the gifts are ours," reads the second verse, "through Him who with us sideth."

I feel as though a miracle has been worked through these many years in my own heart. I think back to those two friends I couldn't invite into our first apartment because it was such a mess, and I know that now the mess wouldn't make any difference. I think of the aching backs from overpreparation for entertaining and compare that now to the ease I experience in arranging a simple evening. I remember my lack of organization, every dish in the cupboard lining the small sink, counter, and cutting board, and I am excited about the systems that have been developed in these years. I consider how my priorities have readjusted, how my attitudes have changed. But most of all I am aware that it is the Holy Spirit who is with me in the planning, in the resting of work. He truly sits with us as we dine, and warms our hearts toward each other.

I can remember the time I winged a skillet across the kitchen to break the tension I felt due to short-notice guests David was bringing home, and I think what a difference the gift of the Holy Spirit can make in our lives. "Your home is filled with peace," said a friend. Yes. It very often is, and that peace is God's.

There is always a quality of surprise that accompanies the use of the gifts of the Spirit. What the Spirit is able to accomplish in us as well as through us is often amazing. We tend to view the work of the supernatural with human eyes, while all the time He is attempting to teach us to view the human with supernatural eyes.

C. S. Lewis has written about this in *Mere Christianity*. "I think that many of us, when Christ has enabled us to overcome one or two sins that were an obvious nuisance, are inclined to feel (though we do not put it into words) that we are now good enough. He has done all we wanted him to do, and we should be obliged if he would leave us alone.

"But the question is not what we intended ourselves to be, but what he intended us to be when he made us . . .

"Imagine yourself as a living house. God comes in to rebuild that house. At first, perhaps, you can understand what He is doing. He is getting the drains right and stopping the leaks in the roof and so on: you knew that those jobs needed doing and so you are not surprised. But presently he starts knocking the house about in a way that hurts abominably and does not seem to make sense. What on earth is he up to? The explanation is

53

that he is building quite a different house from the one you thought of—throwing out a new wing here, putting on an extra floor there, running up towers, making courtyards. You thought you were going to be made into a decent little cottage: but he is building a palace. He intends to come and live in it himself."

How surprised we are to find Him dwelling in the palace He is creating in our lives; and what strange and remarkable gifts He brings to decorate the rooms. These are not to be hoarded or admired, but to be distributed. He paints hospitable pictures within our hearts which we in turn give away through the amazing work of the gift of hospitality.

Life Response

Since prayer is so much the key to developing any gift of the Holy Spirit, here are some "knee" exercises to aid in practicing the gift of hospitality.

1. Wait on the Lord, asking, "Who is it, Lord, to whom You wish me to extend invitation?"

2. Bend your knees to spend time in spiritual heart-reading. Ask yourself: Are there sins in my life I need to confess? Are there people in my life I need to forgive? "These I confess, O Lord, and these I forgive. Create in me a new and clean heart."

3. Take that clean heart along into the hospitality preparations. Remind yourself that it is the Spirit who creates an atmosphere of soul-to-soul, mind-to-mind, heart-to-heart. "Lord, You do the work of spiritual ministry. Help me to keep my human efforts from getting in the way."

5

The Servant

A REPEATED LITANY RINGS FROM THE PENS of the apostles. The letter to the Romans begins, "Paul, a *servant* of Jesus Christ," Philippians introduces, "Paul and Timothy, *servants* of Christ Jesus." The epistle of Titus and the Book of James yield similar proclamations. This theme is echoed again and again– "Simon Peter, a *servant* and apostle of Jesus Christ." It's even included in the last prophetic vision of Scripture, "The revelation of Jesus Christ, which God gave him to show to his *servants* what must soon take place."

Clearly, the apostles understood a concept all but lost to modern Christians. They knew beyond a shadow of doubt that they were servants of Christ and "stewards of the mysteries of God" (I Cor. 4:1). All their service, all their time, all their belongings, all their talents were interpreted in light of the definitive manifesto: You are not your own. You were bought with a price. You are bondslaves of Christ Jesus!

The great stress of Western culture on the individuality of free men, the democratic process, and the inherent right of each to decide his own fate—all tend to obliterate the New Testament concept of servanthood.

A proper restoration of this attitude will greatly alter the way most Christians live. It may call for painful and drastic restructuring of the way we spend our time, of the way we donate our services. But it will also deliver us from the secular me-my mold the world is squeezing us into, as well as from the dominion of the master of mammon. It will have far-reaching implications for our attitudes toward hospitality. When a mind-change has occurred, we will truly be servants of one master, Christ. Our allegiance will be undivided.

Early Christians had less trouble with the slave-servant role because their world was glutted with the actual concept. It has been said that as the modern world is dependent on machine power, the ancient world was dependent upon slavery. Scriptural references to this social system are manifold. The Old Testament chronicles the many facets of slavery. The principle source of slaves was either plunder in war or poverty in peace.

Slavery among the Hebrews broke into the ranks of every human relationship: a father could sell his daughter; a widow's children might be bartered against their father's debts; a man could sell himself. However, legal codes were established to protect the right of the slave as well as the right of the slavemaster, and many of these demonstrated a humaneness beyond that of the surrounding primitive cultures.

The Law provided ways in which a slave could redeem his freedom. He could be purchased by an uncle, by a nephew or cousin, or by any close relative. He was to be freed after the lapse of seven years of servitude and always liberated at the Jubilee year of celebration. If a master caused him permanent physical disability, he was to be released.

Slavery fed the great machine of the Roman empire. It was inhuman in its voracious appetite for bondsmen, yet it provided for the advancement of any who proved to have exceptional intelligence, manual skills, or professional abilities. A common slave could be promoted to the role of steward. Joseph in the Old Testament is an example of the gifted individual wielding authority in his master's name over the household, over an institution, and even over an entire nation. Similar instances may be found in the Roman world.

Jesus Christ colored much of His teachings with references

to this peculiar slave status—that of the one elevated to an uncommon position of responsibility, whose sole intent was to aggrandize the estate of the master. In Luke 12:42, 43, He asks: "Who then is the faithful and wise steward, whom the master will set over his household, to give them their portion of food at the proper time? Blessed is that servant whom his master when he comes will find so doing."

Four chapters later (16:13) He relates the parable of the dishonest steward and begins to instruct His disciples about Christian servanthood. "No servant can serve two masters; for either he will hate the one and love the other, or he will be devoted to the one and despise the other. You cannot serve God and mammon."

Jesus used the parable of the talents (Mt. 25) to construct a framework for correct attitudes toward giving. Here we have an example set for the use of possessions and abilities, and a structure which underlines a basic approach to ministry.

Because Jesus drew comparisons from common life, the disciples gained a lucid concept of their servant relationship to Him. They were thrilled, when, at the end of His life, their Master bestowed upon them an even greater dignity. "No longer do I call you servants . . . but I have called you friends" (Jn. 15:15). They accepted His pronouncement, but they did not presume upon it. The awful events of the following hours emblazoned upon their souls the fact they had been bought with a price—the blood of Christ. They had been ransomed by a near kinsman.

Thus we hear them all declare, "I, Paul; I, Peter; I, Timothy, James, and John—servants of Jesus Christ!" Nothing was given by them outside of this framework; neither money, nor time, nor talent truly belonged to them. Everything was from the Master. Their motivating purpose was to serve and to be found worthy.

How divergent this is from our present employer-employee relationship where work is often terminated at 4:30 p.m. We understand nothing of returning to a home belonging to an employer, to a wife and children owned by him, to being controlled absolutely by one other than ourselves. Culturally, and particularly for those who are white, we are inadequately prepared to understand the steward-master relationship required by the Christian position. We must continually remind ourselves that we contracted an exchange when we knelt before that Cross—my life for His. Spiritual maturity is a continual process of letting go, of submitting to our Head.

I Corinthians 4:2 states, "Moreover it is required of stewards that they be found trustworthy." It is proper to say that the Christian's primary purpose as a steward is to add to the estate of his Master and not to that of his own. All we have belongs to Him—our clothes, our time, our families, our cars, books, inheritances, and homes. Our only consideration should be: How can we best use these for His purposes?

After owning a series of second-hand cars, we were finally able to buy a new model station-wagon tailored for our growing needs—transporting four children, toting people back and forth to meetings, hauling garage-sale finds to refinishers, and bringing home produce from my father's farm.

The first time David used the car for any extensive traveling was to pick up some inner-city kids from camp. While loading them all in the car he caught himself thinking, "Hey! those kids have dirty shoes. They're getting the back all muddy and dirty." Almost instantly came the reminder, *David, that new car isn't yours. It's Mine.*

My husband corrected his attitude, welcomed the gang into the car, and proceeded with the inward dialog: "OK, Lord. If You want Your car dirty and muddy, that's fine with me. I realize it is more important to show love to these, Your children, than to care about this, Your car."

Within an hour of home, he realized that the car was slipping as it automatically shifted from one gear to another. It took so long to accelerate, it became a hazard on the highway. The top

speed slowly seemed to be decreasing—65, 55, 45, finally forlornly limping to our front door at 35.

Certain we had bought a lemon, we returned to the dealer in
our two-week-old car from which we had gained such satisfaction. My husband, however, had learned his lesson well. Why
worry? It was, after all, the Lord's car. "Lord," he prayed,
"this is Your car. You reminded me of that fact when I was
picking up the kids from camp. What are You going to do
about Your car?"

"They put the transmission in wrong in Detroit," the
mechanic informed David. He poured metal shavings into a
container and told us our warranty would cover Detroit's error. The Lord's car has since performed well, taking us 70,000
miles in a few years of traveling with a bare minimum of re-
pairs.

There are benefits to servanthood. The basic one is that the
Lord responds when we practice an attitude of stewardship.
We serve; He then provides the delights of serving. We give,
and He showers upon us His bountiful graces. We bend the
knee in homage, and He lifts us up to rule beside Him.

What a wonderful Master! He is unlike any other. He is
interested equally in all of His stewards. His communication
with His servants is matchless. There is never a time when we
cannot immediately speak to Him, and never an occasion
when His principles regarding life are not available to us.
Those of you who know Him well realize He has a loving sense
of humor. He isn't temperamental. His basic personality
doesn't change from day to day. He is consistent. Our Master,
unlike other masters, is good. In fact, His good is unsurpassed.
He always does the appropriate thing, usually going beyond
what we expect.

He is trustworthy. If He gives His word, even to a slave, you
can expect Him to keep it. Our Master is righteous and just in
the way He operates, and yet He loves us all despite our flaws.
He forgives us again and again, and always goes the extra mile.

He is wise and His wisdom guides us. He helps us past many pitfalls we do not even see. We are stewards—more than that, we are slaves. But unlike other masters, He regards us with fond affection. He calls us His sons and heirs! Perhaps this is because He Himself has been a steward. He humbled Himself, taking on the form of a slave, and therefore can identify closely with us.

He is the wealthiest of all the overlords, and He is the head of all the masters. He is the only one of a kind. He is truly unique, this Master, beyond description!

How can we realize His control in our daily lives? Like many women, I often live in a hectic environment. Recently, with some other women, I spent a weekend in the quietness of a Lutheran deaconess retreat. The cleanliness of the highly waxed floors; the sparkling whiteness of linen cloths; the manicured lawns, with one yard parading old iron clothes poles; the fresh quilted spreads on comfortable beds in garret-like rooms; the bells chiming their precise notifications—all spoke great peace to my soul. I went home determined to bring order into my door-slamming, voices-calling, toy-dominated life!

Monday's work papers were headed in capital letters: PUT ORDER INTO YOUR LIFE—BEGINNING THIS WEEK!! By Thursday my progress was no greater than it had been when the week started. Order eluded me, chased by a growing frustration and resentment at all the interruptions. Tersely I notified a phone-caller (someone in need?), "I just don't have time to talk today. I'm trying to get organized."

Early Friday morning my Master woke me with, *Who do you think you are, ordering your life? You're My servant. You've given yourself to Me. It is I who orders your days and brings order into them.*

It was an old lesson that needed to be relearned. I rose and yielded to Him the order, or lack of it, of my days. Thanking Him for each interruption, I asked only that He make me a fit and useful servant. By 1:30 that afternoon my house was clean, the laundry finished, and I felt as though I had really ministered over the phone to some who had called that day. I spent two hours in His presence and by early evening was ready to leave for a family weekend. The Lord always responds when we practice attitudes of servanthood.

The hardest discipline is learning how to practice these attitudes, discovering means which will render this mindset a habit. Each morning I try to remind myself that I am His servant. A card placed in my Bible or taped by the mirror in the bathroom can serve as an additional notification, "I, Karen Mains, a servant of Jesus Christ."

When I feel the world crowding too close with that certain attitude of wanting, a hungering thing in my heart, then I take a tour of my domain and ask this question: "Whose things are these?" What freedom comes when the answer rises in me: "This is not *my* house but *Yours!* These are not *my* children but *Yours!* These are all a gift from You! You have given them all to benefit Your Kingdom. How can I best employ them for Your service?"

Once we arrive at the attitude of servanthood, we begin the task of establishing priorities. How can I be the best steward of my time? of my abilities? of my finances? of my home? All the areas of our lives must be scrutinized and judiciously juggled. In prayer we have to determine the gifts our Lord wishes us to develop and use; discover which people He wishes us to serve.

We will be forced to make regular checks in order to determine how well we are stewarding. Generally we all have to start with the one great unalterable, time. Am I being a good steward of my time? The only way to discover the answer is to chart one's time, establish a time-log over a specific period of days.

After logging my activities for several weeks, I discovered I was spending more time watching TV than studying Scripture; more time housecleaning than exercising my gifts in ministry; hours were wasted and prayers neglected. Clearly this was not in the interest of my Master! Drastic measures were required: The television was abandoned; prolonged Scripture study and prayer patterns were established. Organized systems of housekeeping were developed, my cleanliness quotient lowered, and a plan for shared work with other family members introduced. These actions, carried out over the period of several months, freed me to participate in the lives of others and develop a deeper relationship with my Lord.

The same evaluation must then be made in other areas of our lives. The use of "my" money should be consistent with my Master's interests. I need to ask, not only, "Does this service my needs and pleasure?" but also, "Does this please my Master?"

Reviewing the major purchases of this last year, we must realize that everything bought really belongs to our heavenly Master. Would our larger investments of the past year please God? Does our regular frittering away of pin money bring credit to His plans? Have I ever budgeted with Him in mind? Are the allocations of my finances under His approval?

Christ speaks of this in Luke 16:11: "If then you have not been faithful in the unrighteous mammon (in regard to money) who will entrust to you the true riches?"

Once we have learned to be stewards on an individual basis, we must begin to consider the corporate implications of servanting. Not only did Christ teach the discipleship of the steward/slave, He expected us to be servants one to another. Our ministry is to be understood in terms of this brand of servanthood.

When the wife of Zebedee requested positions of honor for her sons in the future kingdom, it raised indignation among the other disciples. Jesus used this opportunity to teach them about leadership through serving. "You know that the rulers of the Gentiles lord it over them, and their great men exercise authority over them. It shall not be so among you; but whoever would be great among you must be your servant, and whoever would be first among you must be your slave; even as the Son of man came not to be served but to serve, and to give his life as a ransom for many" (Mt. 20: 25-28).

The last evening of His life He performed a dramatic role-play to insure that they wouldn't forget this hard-won idea. Binding a towel around His waist, He assumed the responsibility of the household slave and washed the dusty, traveled feet of the disciples. "For I have given you an example, that you also should do as I have done to you. Truly, truly, I say to you, a servant is not greater than his master; nor is he who is sent greater than he who sent him" (Jn. 13: 15, 16).

We all know we are to be servants one of another, but making this head-truth a heart-truth is another matter. Ka Tong Gaw, a Filipino who served on the staff of Circle Church for several years, shared a favorite story on learning to be a servant. While attending Bible School in the Philippines, he became disturbed over the conditions of the men's rest rooms— they always seemed to be neglected in the cleaning routine. When nothing was done to correct the filth, he took matters into his own hands and complained to the principal of the school. Imagine his amazement a little later when he saw this same man, mop and pail in hand, slipping from his office into the bathroom. "I thought he would call a janitor, but he cleaned the toilets himself. It was a major lesson to me on being a servant and, of course, raised the question as to why I hadn't taken care of the problem myself."

Often we aren't servants to one another because we haven't allowed the Spirit to sensitize ourselves to one another's cries of need. People say, "I need help," in many different ways. Sometimes these messages are barely audible, fragments of sentences, a look, a sigh. Hearing the meaning behind these whispers demands the highly developed antennae of spiritually mature people.

Unfortunately, most Christians are unable to deal with obvious need. We have discussed many times our inability to respond to the statement, "I need help!" I have always maintained this is not callousness, but inexperience. It is not that we don't want to help, but that we don't know how.

Recently a small group of women in our church were committed to a task demanding extensive work over a year and a half, the joint-effort of which rendered them a close-knit group. One woman, toward the weary but fulfilling end of the project, felt as though she was edging against the reserve of her strength. In that time period she had borne a child, nursed an ailing parent, and ministered in the church. She voiced her need

"You mean no one responded?" I asked when she shared this incident with me, a little amazed because we both respected the depth of the women in the group. She shook her head. "Well, are you sure you expressed your need clearly, so everyone could understand?" I pressed. She had told them she felt she was near a breakdown from exhaustion. The simple point of this is that even these articulate, loving, and sensitive women simply had not heard the cry of help in a way that demanded action.

Often the Lord allows us to experience a time when we express personal need and no one responds. With our last baby, who eventually weighed in, rather come-lately, at 10 lbs. 15 oz., I was so physically miserable I couldn't manage attending church for the last three months of the pregnancy. (My own mother said I was the largest pregnant woman she had ever seen!) During this time only one person called to inquire as to how I was feeling, and no one offered to help me with cleaning chores or with my rambunctious three-year-old. It is true that we were just *learning* how to be servants to one another at the church, rather than *knowing* how to serve one another. But more importantly, the Lord wanted me to examine how often I had failed to serve someone else's need. The question was asked, and I began a spiritual soul-searching, in the quiet of this vacuum, which resulted in deep and lasting changes.

How important it is to develop initiating attitudes of love which ask, "How can I serve?" rather than those gnawing feelings of wanting always to be served by others. In the body of Christ which has truly learned to serve, we find healing for the emotional fragmentation life often delivers to us. Then there comes the day when we discover that part of being a servant is allowing others to minister to us.

Life Response

Explore your abilities in that "foot-washing" kind of service for the body of Christ.

1. Are you ever available for the menial sorts of tasks, or are you forever taking front and center stage?

2. Are you ever filled with joy because people *don't know* it was you who brought love in a special way, or set up the church financial records in that impeccable manner?

3. Think about that one with whom you always seem to have personality clashes. Have you ever attempted to find ways to serve him?

4. What is your attitude when you walk into a room full of people? Are you concerned mostly with what is going to be done for you or what you are going to do for them?

5. If someone asked you how he/she could serve you, would you have ideas to share? Or would you rob the person of an opportunity to model Christ's role of servant toward you?

6

On Serving and Being Served

ONE OF THE UNHEALTHY SYNDROMES which often develops in the clergy is an unstated attitude of, "I'm here to help you, you're not here to help me." It is rarely that crassly stated, but is usually subconsciously communicated. Ministers, as well as their congregations, need to realize that ministry is a two-way enterprise. Even the strongest have moments when they need a loving shoulder.

Frequently, and sometimes justly, David and I have been accused of always being so busy helping other people that we were unable to receive help ourselves. You *can* discipline yourself so strictly that putting other people first becomes a habit, and a good one. Upon entering a crowded room, you immediately think, "Who here is needing love or encouragement? Who is lonely? Who is hurting?" You pattern yourself to find the sensitive ways to respond. You concentrate on giving. Consequently, you become almost unable to recognize, let alone express, your own needs.

We have often had to stop ourselves and inquire, "Now what needs do *we* have? And how can we allow others to serve us?" Generally, most of the things on our lists were services requiring specialized skills of mechanics and carpenters and electricians rather than emotional and psychological helps. Sometimes this was frustrating for those to whom we had given emotional support. They wanted to return like for like.

We all need to learn to give what we are able to, and never to downgrade the gifts God has imparted to us. I have been as deeply ministered to by people fixing my plumbing as by those who have stood beside me in moments of soul crises.

Even the strong have moments of shattering weakness, when listening ears and understanding hearts, soft voices and sympathetic responses are required. Each of us at some time should experience the taste of weakness. On one occasion both David and I found our capacities drained. Simply overworked, we were in an unstated race as to who would go over the edge first. Committed to tasks beyond our strength, we kept looking for the Lord to provide the needed energy. He did. He allowed me to slip over the precipice into the chasm. It wasn't a tearing, crashing, screaming sort of fall; just a slipping from hand-hold to hand-hold with bits of dislodged earth crumbling down with my own descent. An abutment kept me from breaking on the floor of the canyon's bottom; and I rested there for a while (about six months) feeling bruised and shaken and slightly ashamed I had walked so foolhardily on the cliff.

For weeks I had gone to bed each night aching with physical tiredness. A demanding counseling load, daily household management, concern over David's exhaustion, overdue writing commitments—all seemed to require everything I had to give. One afternoon I lunched with a friend, then hurried on to shop for some baby gifts. I kept experiencing short, blank pauses in the bargain basement of Marshall Field's when I couldn't remember where I was or what I was doing there. I had a terrible impression that if I stayed longer, I wouldn't be able to remember who I was, either. It was time to quit.

Leaving without buying a thing, I caught public transportation, dragged myself home, and announced, "I need three things: I need rest. I need quiet. I need to be taken care of." David called a doctor from the church, and her husband, who is a psychological counselor. They came, diagnosed a stress reaction, and I went to bed.

I learned a myriad of lessons from this experience, which eventually stretched through a vacation into a three-month sabbatical for us. The basic lesson, of course, was that we all corporately, including the minister and his family, need to be serving one another. If the total body is exercising its gifts, not so much falls on the shoulders of the professional clergy who have a tendency to overload anyway.

Second, we learned we need to let go of those things which can't be done. It is simple but difficult to realize that the Lord is the Head of the church. We are stewarding on His behalf within it. If there are personnel or program gaps, it is His problem.

At the time of my plummeting, we were in the middle of important church structural changes. We had to remove ourselves during critical months of restructuring and commit to the hands of other faithful stewards this strategic work. Returning from our sabbatical, we found they had exercised their gifts beautifully. Stars, bars, and merit awards! The Lord was capable of working in His church through other abilities than our own. It was a truth we knew but needed to radically experience. We were forced to let go, and others were forced to pick up. The strength we required was supplied through the corporate health of our functioning body.

For those several months I learned to cry, "Help! Help!" A full gamut of loving ministry was extended to me; and I allowed myself to become dependent, for that while, upon what I received. The Enemy had probably intended this incident for bad, but the Lord as usual used it for good in our lives.

We are servants of Christ and servants within His body. We need to learn to hear articulate and inarticulate cries for help. We need to develop our capacities for service. We need to be aware that whenever we are serving one another, there is always the possibility of new and fearful situations. Our insecurities arise to assail us. "Should I do this? Should I call? Won't I just be bothering them? Will that person be offended if

69

I offer to help? Is this the Spirit telling me to do this, or is this my own flesh goading me into trouble?"

Several years back, one of the women in the congregation delivered her first baby stillborn. We were all sorry and someone said to me, "I feel so badly for Sheri. I wanted to write a note and tell her so but I hardly know her." I could understand those feelings since I had experienced them often myself.

A few weeks later I was talking to Sheri and she commented on the support she had received from the people in the church. "You know," she remarked, "I received a note from Mary (another woman). It meant so much to me because I hardly know her, and to think she would care enough to take the time to sit down and write!"

Every pastor's wife finds herself in the center of the lives of her congregation receiving information juxtaposed against other information. Sometimes we know things we shouldn't know, but at other times we learn from experiences we don't have to go through. I determined, from this instance of note writing, to always initiate love, to attempt to refuse the flutters of fear which appear in new circumstances of ministry. If an idea seems to be good, I concluded, it is most probably of God, and I will attempt to do it. Fear is generally a tool the Enemy uses to keep us from touching each other with the healing ointment of love. We must learn to initiate love even when we have not been asked to do so, even when there is no return, or when we are not sure how people will respond.

Sensitivity to cries for help is the work of the Spirit. The proper functioning of our gifts is the work of the Spirit. Learning to ask for help, learning how to give it—He is the tutor in these things.

If we truly develop stewardship attitudes toward our possessions, and if we then become servants one of another, we must expect the quality of our life together as Christians to be enhanced. The women in one church asked: Can we as stewards really justify the time and money we spend in the pursuit of fashion? They established a clothing co-op where excess, usable garments could be exchanged, and where children's clothes could be traded. Then they had enough of a sense of togetherness not to be embarrassed at wearing each other's hand-me-downs on Sunday morning.

If my time doesn't belong to me but to my Master for use in His Kingdom, this is bound to have a bearing on the way I utilize my fleeting moments of earthly tenure. Learning that He orders my days was a valuable lesson. I try to seek His will for this day in my life. For many years my job has been to minister to the body of Circle Church. That along with the serving of my husband and family was, as far as I understood it, my priority. Sometimes the combination of both, of keeping each in alignment, created tensions. Someone weeping in the living room (or as one of my neighbors expressed it, "Just one of [those] people the Mainses are always having over") demanded my attention as much as the little boys feuding in the back yard.

Despite the pastoral responsibilities, the physical functions of life go on. Laundry must be stuffed into machines, toys jammed away into drawers and shelves, meals economically planned and prepared, dishes scrubbed, rooms straightened. Sometimes these material basics can be in hot competition with the needs of church and family. I came to learn to cry out to the Lord, "You see what needs to be done in this house. You order my days."

Invariably, when I pray this prayer, then cast myself into the day with this attitude, He does order them. I may be in the middle of what seems to be an important project—paint cloths spread and brushes dripping for the color accent on the living room wall—the phone interrupts and the paint dries forlornly on the applicator. Who is in control of my time? I ask. (He orders my days. If that project is important He will provide the way to finish it.) How many times can I testify to His giving me a welcoming and listening ear for callers, giving me patience as well as delight in my children, making me an eager companion for my husband. He orders the days, clears the frustrations; He brings someone to offer aid, or a word of encouragement.

This year my priority is a writing ministry. He continues to order these days by providing circumstances which have so limited me that I have been unable to commit myself to long-term person-to-person ministry. Others have picked up those responsibilities, freeing me for writing, my family, and short one-to-one counseling. The phone has been quieter during these months than ever in our lives!

When we understand that He is Lord of our time, we realize that interruptions are of His planning. They become opportunities to serve rather than plagues to keep us from functioning. We begin to experience the surprising miracle of living in the center of His will.

When we have developed the mindset of a steward toward our possessions we will view them not as this-is-mine-I-worked-hard-for-it, but as tools to unite the body—a home for prayer groups, cars for transporting kids to parties, coffee servers to share for large groups—instruments given to us by our Master for service in His Kingdom.

Realizing we live in a high crime society, I nevertheless see the closed and locked doors of our churches as a statement of possessiveness—this is our church, we have worked hard for it, we don't want anything unseemly to happen here. Couldn't alternate plans be arranged so little-used sanctuaries would be available like the cathedrals in Europe for continual prayer pilgrimages? How little quiet there is in this frenetic world. How few places for protected peace. We really do need to be offering sanctuary to secular society, opened doors to troubled hearts.

The fact that so many of our church buildings sit empty for major portions of the week perhaps poses questions of stewardship. Can we really justify spending such time and expense in building these structures which are only used a few hours weekly? If they are strictly for show or convenience, is this expenditure really in the interest of our Master? Are there ways we can make our facilities more functional? Are there community services we can perform which will demonstrate Christlikeness to this world? Can we, perchance, do without a building?

When we are servants, our hospitality takes on different dimensions. Our homes are used to build one another, to bind ourselves together—not to create barriers of needless competition or comparisons. We can provide healing when we offer to one another small refuges from the battle. I can testify to being positively mellow for days after spending an evening in the home of those who extended their gift of hospitality. Walking away from some doors, I have carried with me a special feeling of being cherished, comforted. Contrasted to this was the evening we spent in one home where all the details were correct, the rooms beautifully appointed, the table cleverly arranged—but where our hostess criticized the work we were doing for a major portion of the night. It took several days to recover from the emotional fatigue this encounter engendered. She was clearly not exercising a gift—not even one of exhortation!

A reluctance to leave, a feeling of warmth toward each other, the catharsis of laughter and sometimes singing or prayer—these are what we receive due to another's service; and if the food has been well prepared or creatively served, so much the better. But it is the quality of our relationships which counts. We find we have given each other the Spirit of Christ, a taste of His love, a mirror of His care, a candle-flicker of His face. We have used our gifts as stewards. We have served and been served by one another. May we now know His approval in our efforts. May we with eager anticipation look to that day when we hear His voice, "Well done, good and faithful servant; you have been faithful over a little, I will set you over much; enter into the joy of your master" (Mt. 25:23).

Life Response

1. How would your Master rate your servanthood? If you were to meet with Him in a quiet evaluation session, what mark would He give you for your attitudes of stewardship in the following four areas?

The use of your time:

Poor   Fair   Good   Excellent

The distribution of your money:

Poor   Fair   Good   Excellent

The use of your home:

Poor   Fair   Good   Excellent

The use of your possessions:

Poor   Fair   Good   Excellent

What kind of changes do you think He might require in the areas where He rated you poorly? What kind of priorities will you have to set up in your low-rated areas in order to establish a Kingdom mindset?

7

Telltale Marks

THE MUD MARKS SWAGGERED BOLDLY across the gold carpet, marched around the freshly washed kitchen tile, meandered down the hall, stopped at the bathroom sink—then ended in scattered clods of earth on the porch and down the front steps. It all must have happened in the space of my quick dash to a "borrowing neighbor."

"Joel! Jo-el Da-vid!" I called. My mother-mind had quickly assessed to which culprit the mud marks belonged: the great house despoiler, Joel David Mains. Two small figures came bounding joyously from the back yard, their snowsuits besotted and begrimed—my son and his pal Georgie. Georgie is five, but in stature he is eight, causing him to lope and stumble like an adolescent puppy.

"What have you been doing?" I demanded.

"Playing in the back yard," came the reply.

"No! No! What have you been doing in my house? There's mud from front to back!" I cried.

Innocently, both boys checked their boots. All four were huge clods of clay properly cemented to moldering fall leaves.

"It was Georgie," maintained the ever-loyal Joel. "It was Joel," countered Georgie, a little slower on the draw.

Obviously chagrined by a mother who would make so much over such a minor incident, Joel volunteered more information. "Georgie/just/wanted/a/glass/of/water." Each word was

75

pronounced in a separate, distinct tone, in a manner reserved for communication with the deaf, the infirm, or the half-wit.

"Well," I replied, also being deliberately distinct, "the next time Georgie wants a glass of water, tell him to/get/it/in/his/own/house." And having had the last word, I dismissed them.

Within minutes, aided by a wet rag and vacuum, I erased the telltale evidences. Glancing at the clock I discovered that two lovely hours remained before the older children arrived home from school. Grabbing my Bible, I crept past the baby's door listening for the reassuring pattern of his breathing, then on to my very own place—a seat beneath the big window where I can see the sky, blue or gray. A little hurriedly I whispered, "Here I am again, Lord. It's Karen. What have You to teach me today?"

Opening the Scripture, I continued my synoptic study of the Gospels. Certain vibrant phrases stood forth. "If, as my representatives, you give even a cup of cold water to a little child, you will surely be rewarded . . ." and "Anyone who takes care of a little child is caring for God who sent me. Your care for others is the measure of your greatness."

Shame flooded me. *Georgie just wanted a glass of water.* I bowed my heart and prayed, "Father, forgive me for caring more for clean floors and tidy schedules than for two little boys."

Suddenly I remembered a voice from the past—Linda's as she leaned across the high school lunch table. "Does your mother always sing around the house like that—like I heard her singing when we were talking on the phone yesterday?" When I answered that she did, Linda looked at me and with envy said, "You're so lucky!"

The world is full of Georgies just wanting a drink of water, and of Lindas, wishing they had mothers who sang in the kitchen. Many of them are our children's friends. We really have no choice—we who know the One who is the Living Water, this same One who creates new songs in our hearts—

we have no choice but to open our homes and our lives to those who may leave their telltale marks.

Why is it always easier to extend the courtesies of hospitality to those outside our immediate families? Husbands, housemates, children, or strangely enough, their friends, often receive short shrift of our kindly attention. This point was brought forcibly home to me by my daughter, who cleverly exclaimed before a roomful of guests, "Mommy, why aren't you this nice to us when people *aren't* here?"

Hospitality like charity, in order to be true, has to begin at home. The Lord has humiliated me enough through the comments of my own children that I have been forced to examine my attitudes toward them. Did it count, all this gracious open-house business, if I acted like a hellion the hour before company arrived? Wasn't there something hypocritical about receiving laurels for my church work if my own children's friends were neglected? Wasn't there a glaring inconsistency if I really treated my children differently when outsiders were around? Through the years I had come to an understanding of the use of hospitality as a gift of the Holy Spirit for ministry. But was I really ministering to my own?

A woman can't be perfect in everything, can she? Yet telltale marks had been imprinted on my own heart by the timely reading of the Scripture verse: *If you give even a cup of cold water to a little child . . . anyone who takes care of a little child is caring for God who sent me.*

"Let's be friends," said a certain three-year-old, intruding his pug nose and snuggling his body under the covers to interrupt my slumber. Opening my eyes to the morning sunlight flooding the bedroom, I thought regretfully of yesterday's battles. Then, placing a kiss—half on hair and half on cheek—I whispered back, "Yes, let's be."

His little plea reinforced the theme of an article written by a psychologist on child rearing which I had recently read. "Be friends with your children," the expert had advised. "Treat

77

them the same way you would your friends."

I began to ask myself, "How would I say that to a friend?" and found my attitudes of annoyance mellowing. How often I've harangued, "Hang up your coat. Pick up your toys. If I've told you once, I've told you a million times, etc., etc." To a friend I would probably suggest, "There are hooks in the hall. Would you like to hang your coat in there?"

Don't my children (and husband and parents and room-mates) deserve the same special consideration I show to a friend? When a friend walks through that door, my attitude is one of greeting, of welcome. Children, however, are often blasted with, "You didn't put the peanut butter away after lunch. Wipe your feet. Take your books off the dining room table." After taking time to temper my commands with kind-ness, after discovering ways to communicate as well as feel friendship, I was amazed at the speed with which I was obeyed. The sharp edge of commands began to ease into a sweetly nectared agreement.

Upon honestly examining my attitudes, how often I found myself relieved to be relieved of my children. Now each of us deserves a certain measure of privacy, but there are some parents who seem to hate to be in the same house with their own children. Yet, I love to be with my friends. True, they aren't always underfoot making strident demands; but if I learn to be a friend to my children, can't they in turn learn to be a friend to me?

I thought back to my own parents. I can't remember them not conveying total enjoyment of me. There were moments of discipline, but the general tone of our relationship was one of mutual enjoyment. I recall comments like, "Find something quiet to do," but only because I am now saying those things to my own children! The words out of the past I most readily hear are, "Please come along with us. We just want to have your company."

My "childness" was never used as an excuse to dismiss me

78

from adult conversations. When asked about this, my mother usually replies, "You were never a child!" She's right, because she herself bestowed upon me the honor of companionship.

My husband and I are working hard to create this atmosphere of closeness in our own family. He has established a special tradition of taking one child to early breakfast alone. Great secrets are shared, marvelous private communications occur at these outings. We are trying to make the times we do spend as a family unit lovely—filled with laughter and games, wrestling and sharing, growing and becoming. The TV has had to go for many reasons, but one of them was that it cut into the companionship of our family times.

Friends talk with each other. They share intimately on private levels. It is easy for our communication with our children to degenerate to the degree of no more than, "Where are you going; what are you doing?" Efforts have to be made to extend our talks to, "What are you thinking; how do you feel about this?"

I discovered early that my taciturn eldest child became positively garrulous before bedtime. If it was a ploy to stall the ending of day, it worked because I was so charmed by the rare and satisfactory moments provided by his tactics. Thoughts about God, fears and feelings, happy teasing—all were shared gems to me. We have, each of us, a "talking place." How lovely to enter there and find someone we love waiting with a listening ear.

It is frightening how few of us communicate the most important things to our children—the spiritual things. Do my children know when and how my own conversion took place, or what I am learning in this daily relationship with my Lord, or what portions of Scripture have become meaningful to me? Am I exercising my gifts of the Holy Spirit in ministry in my own home? Am I teaching my children the deeper meaning of friendship, that of being brothers and sisters in Christ?

"Let's be friends," I said the other day to that three-year-old, now ten. (I am learning some lessons.) We were in a nose-to-nose confrontation—the garbage was moldering in its container. Conflict was in the air, but with those words it began to dissipate. He relaxed his forehead against my own, locked his arms lightly around my neck, and whispered back, "Yes, let's be!"

How often we overlook the needs of our own children, even those of the children of our own churches. Busy with adult conversations, with grown-up preoccupations, we are more concerned that they not run between the pews than about the condition of their impressionable spirits. Looking back to my home church, I realize it was not the adults that acted as substitute parents during my teen years who impressed me the most; rather it was those who stopped to inquire about my thoughts, who praised me for a special accomplishment, who demonstrated some aspect of vital Christianity—those who gave consideration to me *when I was a child*.

Both sets of grandparents live geographically close, and David and I are grateful for the input and interest they can give to our children. Each family has different activities they enjoy, unique perspectives from which their grandchildren can draw deeply. In addition to this personal wealth, we are discovering the bounty of the extended family of our church community. The benefits derived from the attention of other adults toward our children are invaluable.

Just recently the older children were invited to go fossil hunting in a stone quarry with another family from the church. They returned, knees skinned and baskets filled with archaic treasures pressed in rock, enthusiastic about this new interest. That same week a single friend took the smaller boys on a fishing trip, then was talked into setting up his tarpaulin in the back yard for a one-night sleeping tent. Since my husband's interest in camping runs more to the hotel/motel variety, this is an experience for the children we welcome.

We are working diligently to remind ourselves that the church is in reality an extended family and that we all bear responsibility for the nurturing of the children of this body. Singles also benefit from these relationships. Seeking oneness in Christ in a world which places undue emphasis on coupling can be a hazardous task, but it is often eased by the eager, loving response of someone else's children. How often I have heard people express thankfulness for the physical contact. To be able to hug and wrestle and touch, wholesomely and without societal disapproval, is a healing encounter provided by children who will readily exchange "scrunches and smooches."

This is such a Christlike quality, this hospitality toward children. It is not simply a matter of being open toward our own, difficult as that often is, but it requires that we accept, encourage and want those born of someone else, whether we are married or not, whether we have children of our own or not. The story of Christ blessing the children is not only for the nursery but for adult Sunday school as well. If He could welcome the interruption of His ministry by wiggling, wonderstruck, bouncing, impertinent humanity, can we dare do less? Unless we come to know children, how can we deeply understand the meaning of His words, "Except ye become as little children, ye cannot enter the Kingdom of Heaven." Childlikeness is a quality to be cultivated in our maturity—trust, dependency, anticipation, a sense of wonder. We can give much to those small people of our churches, but they can give more to us.

This year's clean-your-desk-at-school junk included a notebook in which my daughter and her teacher had written correspondence over the period of several months. I imagine he had established this with his class in order to encourage not only writing skills but communication. Some of the comments are hilarious, others poignant. An interesting item was written on Tuesday, March 2.

Melissa:	*I think adults would be the best.*
	I think it would be the best because we have comany a lot. We also have to go to are aunts house alot. Thats why I say adults would be the best.
Teacher:	Why?
Melissa:	*I said because we have lots of adults over. And all so that we go to are parents friends house alot. It says it right up there. We go to my moms mom house to.*

Needless to say, I was left with a warm feeling after reading this. For those of us who have lived through the generation whose rallying cry was once "Don't trust anyone over 30!" it is good to feel that Melissa truly does think adults would be the best. Her relationships so far with older people have been satisfactory, she is not afraid of the time to come, or of those who people that region of life. Her trust is intact.

Maturity has often been defined as feeling at home with people of all ages. What better preparation for growing up could I possibly give to these children than that comfortable acceptance of people who are older. This is one of the reasons we particularly cherish the adults who are our children's friends—they are assisting, through light camaraderie or special-interest projects, in the process of maturation.

Recently the Lord has convicted me that my largest lack in hospitality is toward my own children's friends. Telltale marks indeed—it was hard to open my cleaned rooms to toy-oriented hands and feet. My own knew they were expected to pick up after themselves, but this standard was a little harder to impose on the neighbors' kids.

Coming downstairs one day, arms loaded with soiled sheets

and blankets, I nudged my way around two little forms hud-
dled in conference on the treads. *Why do children love stairs
so much?* Excusing myself, we shifted positions a bit, and I
balanced my load on its way to the washer in the basement. I
had not gone too far when I heard a little voice pipe, "I love to
come to your house. Your mother doesn't yell all the time the
way my mother does."

It gave me pause, and I suddenly realized this little girl had
been around frequently. I didn't know her mother so I hadn't
any way to judge the comment about yelling, but I did sense
she had found shelter, a quiet space in a noisy world. *You are
welcome, child, to my stairway any time.*

The second incident occurred during a premarital counseling
session. The bridegroom-to-be was an excellent artist with
heightened sensitivity, but while investigating his family
background we realized there seemed to be nothing which
would have opened the perceptions of a young child to the
beauties of the world around him. In more than one way, he
was a miracle of God's grace.

Intrigued, we prodded more into the past, searching for
those relationships which might have unfolded his potential
and nurtured his rare talent—an art teacher? a distant relative?
He smiled, remembering something good. "I had a girl
friend," he explained. "And her mother belonged to a Great
Books discussion group. She would talk about ideas, litera-
ture, things never mentioned in my own home. It was the first
time I knew anyone who was interested in what I thought, who
expected me to have opinions and ideas. After a while, I think
I just dated the girl to be in her home."

Thinking back to the teens of my own high school I wondered how many of them could have been stimulated by the
shelter of my home. The dinner-table talk was lively—we
didn't think it was any good unless someone disagreed. There
was music, lots of laughter, security. I can recall the sense of
urgency with which I hurried home after school. The most

exciting and interesting things happened in my own home: there were phone messages or the accounts of my parents' activities, and I was always eager to resume my place near the center of them. If only somehow I could have shared this wealth with those teens whose heels dragged reluctantly homeward. One of the few regrets I have about growing up was that my parents were both too busy (each had demanding professional positions) to help me extend the circumference of our circle of warmth toward my nonchurch friends.

Though I continually absorbed stirring challenges to witness, I was nevertheless woefully inadequate and frequently doctored myself with lethal doses of guilt. Witness, to me in those days, consisted of refraining from an endless list of evils, carrying my Bible daily on top of my schoolbooks, grabbing honors in order to be respected, and cramming verbal testimony into conversations whenever the opportunity permitted. I knew nothing of heartfelt empathy, of sensing despair and loneliness in the lives of my classmates, of giving to them the ministry of Christ and thereby paving the way for valid witness. My own faith was barely a hard nub of a bud near opening.

How often do we as adults expect our children to do in their world what we fail to do in our own? I wonder now how many unloved teens there were in the corridors of that school, how many with the souls of artists who would have flourished in the environments of Christian homes. *Help me, Lord, to remember what little attention it takes to open the eyes of youth to the glories of the world and to the Kingdom which exists.*

We are on the verge of the teen years in our home. I am tempted to draw these my children behind the protection of our several walls, to raise my banner of isolationism against this crass society. Yet my head knows it is sin to close the doors of this fortress with ourselves safely inside. I must swing open those hinges and allow my offspring to forage and explore. I only hope we have made them feel so welcome in these early years that they will want to hurry home and bring the friends they've discovered home as well.

After resolving to develop more hospitality in this area, we took some of the children's friends to a church picnic where the afternoon activities included eating and games as well as a baptismal service in the polluted muck of the Fox River. (Some of us concluded that if the dirty Jordan cured Naaman of his spots, this water must be performing untold wonders for those being immersed in it!) Testimonies were given, and many strangers gathered on the banks drawn by their curiosity. Despite the environment, it was a lovely ceremony, due perhaps to the fact that many were new Christians.

Afterward, my oldest child Randy's friend, whose customary approach to the world is bravado (and who, I suspect, suffers some of the complications of a broken home), announced, "Well, Mrs. Mains. I've decided that next year I'm going to be baptized. Now my family's not a Christian background, but I'm a Christian, and I think I should be baptized." We will explore, of course, to see how deeply the Spirit is working in this heart, but, oh, how easy to open youth's eyes to the Kingdom.

Looking into that face framed by shaggy bangs, I prayed, *O Lord, firm my heart in its resolve to be open to these my children's friends. Don't let me be frightened by the world's intents. Help me to keep the hinges open, and the towers strong, and the fires inside warm and bright. By the grace of your Son. Amen.*

When children live in a hospitable home, they begin to share the telltale marks. Not only do they learn the tools of hospitality—clearing tables, filling water glasses, greeting people at the door, taking coats, finding toys for younger guests—they become familiar with the spirit as well.

Conversation, for example, becomes a natural art. How many times in the middle of some discourse have I felt a little body snuggle into my chair. Subdued is the mouth, but open are the ears. Like my mother, I don't believe in excluding children on the general principle that they are children. I remember with great fondness those tales woven on the looms of my ancestors' past; the amazing recognition that my father could talk to anyone about anything; the joy I felt when adults laughed together. If the evening is flowing, and the children's behavior suitable, they are welcome to listen and to learn to participate.

Naturally, there are times when, because of the intimacy of the subject, or because of the late hour, the children are excused. Often they have other pursuits which are more intriguing. Yet it is not unusual to have a child's arm dangling over the back of my ladder chair, a small head pressing cheek to cheek, a hand squeezing out the nonverbal plea, "It's all right if we stay, isn't it?" What better way for children to learn to converse than by observing this lively art.

One evening after the late-night company had departed, we climbed the stairs to make our regular bedcheck. All four beds were empty—even the toddler's crib! Conducting a household bodyhunt, we finally located the four soundly asleep beneath the large round table in the living room, hidden by its long cloth. They had crept downstairs and, unseen by any of the guests, crawled behind the benches and curtains to this covert, each trailing a pillow along! There, lulled by laughter and muted tones, they drifted into dreams, still feeling they were a part of the comfort of our circle.

Still deeper effects have been worked in their lives by our hospitality to people in need. I have often been asked how our children have been influenced by the fact that David and I do so much counseling in our home with people in distress, and that we have even invited some to live with us for a while. My answer is that the influences seem to be only positive.

It's nothing to grab a child as he scoots through the hall and send him off for a box of tissues for someone's tears. They are learning not to be afraid of people's problems, but are realizing that human suffering is a part of living. They seem not to be surprised upon encountering it. In fact, I think they are better for knowing we can help one another despite the tears.

We are continually complimented (and this is one of the rich payoffs to parenting—other people's evaluations) on the children's maturity. I'm sure much of this is due to their being comfortable with adults, but I think much of it must be attributed to the fact that they are becoming sensitized to others' suffering. Teachers often comment that one of the children has a heightened sense of justice, an awareness of what is right, which is coupled with a compassion displayed in the classroom or on the playground. Our children are richer for living in an open house. Hopefully, it will prepare them to face their own griefs in the days ahead and to share in the pains of the world around them.

I can remember the time my back door opened and a grubby boot threatened to descend in ruinous contact with my kitchen floor. (Why the former tenant of the house who filled the place with eight sons would choose white tile for her decorating scheme is beyond me. All I can conclude is she must have been a wonder in courage!) Impatience welled, but an inward voice spoke first. *Be careful what you say.* Look into those eyes. Don't you see that Christ has come into your kitchen— "Anyone who takes care of a little child is caring for God who sent me."

The foot came down on the floor, and I knew at that moment this was going to be a hard discipline, this seeing Christ in those of my immediate family, in those who would leave their telltale marks over my floors and plans and life. A difficult discipline?—yes, but it is a worthy one. If I give to them but a cup of water, Christ counts it as unto Himself. I am not only called to minister to my church or to my world, but I am privileged to serve those with whom I live. This concept has elevated my role of mother and wife and housemate to one of extreme satisfaction, but it has also made me greatly aware of the daily Presence of Christ who, after all, leaves some telltale marks of His own in our souls.

> Christ be with me, Christ within me,
>   Christ behind me, Christ before me,
> Christ beside me, Christ to win me,
>   Christ to comfort and restore me,
> Christ beneath me, Christ above me,
>   Christ in quiet, Christ in danger,
> Christ in hearts of all that love me,
>   Christ in mouth of friend and stranger.
>   ST. PATRICK OF IRELAND

Life Response

Look closely at those with whom you come in contact. Are there ways you can be more Christlike in serving them?

1. *Your own children.* Which telltale marks are most annoying? The infant's diapers? The toddler's toys? The Little Leaguer's bats and mitts and balls? The daughter's whirlwind collection of dolls and miniature garments? The teen's preference for music?

2. *Your children's friends.* Are the phone calls which come during dinner telltale marks? What about that certain abrasive personality?

3. *Your friend's children.* Have you ever thought, "If you were my child, you would never get away with—"? How would Christ treat this personality?

4. *The children in the neighborhood.* Do you know their names? Have you ever taken time to talk with them?

5. *The children in your church.* Do you love them as though they were your own? Do you feel any responsibility to contribute to their growth?

6. *The child you have never seen before.* Who knows what bruises or wounds, marks of another sort, are being inflicted on this soul. One with runny nose, dirty clothes, impertinent personality—what of Christ can you contribute to this one you may never see again?

8

Welcome

I love the story of the elderly woman who was touring several guests through her latest upstairs redecorating project. Upon hearing her husband return home after a day's work, she excused herself with the words, "Pardon me for a moment while I run downstairs to greet Andrew. I never like him to return home without welcoming him." Through decades of marriage now stretched into the autumn of life, through thousands of homecomings, this woman had preserved her spirit of greeting. What a warm relationship had evolved here over the many years!

Perhaps more difficult than developing attitudes of welcome

toward our children is keeping a spirit of invitation open toward those adults with whom we live—husbands, roommates or parents.

Hospitality toward the adults with whom we live is more, of course, than dropping things to rush with a greeting toward the front door. Yet this moment of homecoming is often an accurate thermometer which gauges what we truly feel toward our housemates. In fact, I suspect that the quality of our front-door reception can greatly determine the atmosphere of that afternoon and evening's life together. It wouldn't hurt us to adopt some of the essence of mythical or classic drama where toga-clad or befurred men and women lift hands and voices to cry, "Hail! Therastinor, son of Midian, King of Numinor—" Extreme? Well, yes. But something within must rush to salutation. We need to ask: Is it good to join company again after a day apart? Do we give entrance to our homes and hearts to each other?

My husband has always been pleased when the children rushed, jumped, almost wagged their greetings. The cries can often be heard up and down the block. "Daddy's home! Daddy's home! Daddy! Daddy!" Here again we adults need to learn something of childlikeness and extend to one another similar glad greetings. There is sorrow enough in this workaday world; there is grinding a-plenty. Home is the place we should return to with eager spirits, the journey's end we reach with sighs of contentment.

Sadly, few of us create homes for each other. The fact that people can live together under the same roof and maintain hour after hour of chilly silence is a mystery to me. Something inwardly whispers *outrage*. The fact that even Christians can commit this abomination against communion is despicable. We must learn to share our lives, to intermingle thoughts and emotions, and to thereby consecrate our tiny dwellings in this large world as a place in which His Presence is pleased to abide. Disunity is a sure sign that He has not been allowed to become a guest within our inner beings, and therefore has no place in our material abodes either. The world needs models. We must, for its sake if no other, institute hostels of love and of peace. We need to flesh out the trite "there's a welcome here," by affirming it in our lives together before we try to extend it to the society at large.

All of our homes, whether those of married people, of single roommates, or of singles and marrieds joining in community (which is happening more frequently) have the same positive potential. Each household has the option of creating family. A marriage license is not a written guarantee that relationships will flourish. Our counseling calendar as well as the secular statistics have amply proven that a ceremony and shared bed with resultant offspring do not a family make.

The word family holds for me connotations of closely bonded ties, loyalty deeper than understanding, an almost mystical rapprochement, support unto death, unfaltering acceptance, ready encouragement, sustaining and comforting love. I am aware that I expect a great deal from this relationship. And I know that the life experiences of many have forced them to think of family in completely opposite terms—competition, jealousy, haranguing, lack of acceptance, even bitter hatred. It is important to understand, therefore, for synoptical reasons, the significance I attach to the term. I truly believe that whenever we gather together under one roof, be it in a dormitory, a community, or a singular dwelling, we have the opportunity of creating family.

Whether this occurs or not is a matter of choice and discipline. We choose whether to make our household relationships rich and rewarding, cherishing and trusting—or the opposite. Our attitude is what determines if that rare miracle of closeness will occur. We all—husband and wife, career girls living together, medical students sharing an apartment—have the opportunity of forming this miraculous unit.

"But married people can live together because they love one

93

another. It's different for us," I can hear some unmarrieds exclaim. Yet the media testify to millions of unhappy marriages and prove often enough that a legal marriage ceremony seems almost a guarantee that love will flee. We all need to comprehend that love doesn't just happen, it is made. When we work at it, then it grows; but it never flourishes in neglect.

David and I have both heard each other declare adamantly that if anything happened to the other we would never marry again, and surrounded by cloudy foresight, we both agree. This declaration is made despite the fact that our marriage has been uncommonly happy and definitely fulfilling. Yet the effort required to make it so has been so incredible we both doubt whether we could justify the time taken from Kingdom work that would be necessary to render another as satisfying. The Apostle Paul had valid reasons for recommending singleness. Good communication involves hours of work. Understanding is an art which must be fostered. Real empathy takes years to develop; and love does not spontaneously sustain itself over the living together of days, but must be gardened— hoed, weeded and watered.

I can remember as a young bride those moments of terror when I realized I felt no love in my heart for my husband. It became very real to me at those times how easily love flees. I learned early in marriage that the human heart is a vessel not large enough to sustain love. Kneeling is the proper position for discovering love again. How often I came to my Heavenly Father and pleaded, "Lord, I just don't feel any love for David. Fill me, please, with your supernatural grace for Him." There I found the source that is beyond all human effort, the everlasting, long-suffering love of God. "Oh, give thanks to the Lord, for he is good; his lovingkindness continues forever" (Ps. 136:1, TLB).

Continually He filled the cup of my young soul. Into this endless well I have learned to dip my bucket, and in the refreshment of its long draughts breathe then a loving atmosphere into our home. As my husband does the same, we are able to establish the miracle of family.

It is important to realize that family is not the prerogative of the married, and love is not exclusive to this relationship. I am adamantly opposed to the old saw that "there are just some people we can't love." We can all learn to practice love toward one another. Anything less for the Christian borders on heresy, because it defies the power of God's Spirit in our lives and flails against the promises of Scripture. Christ's new commandment is valid for us today. We are to love one another as He loved us, and by this shall the world know that we are His disciples.

Love is action with feeling and feeling with action. There isn't anyone His Spirit can't create this combination in my heart toward if I ask Him. I say this after personally struggling to love many unlikely people and after having discovered the amazing resources of God.

A Christian family should become a microcosm of the church. We need to set about to create within our families *an atmosphere of devotion*. The healthy vital signs—meaningful prayer, heart-lifting worship, shared fellowship around our common faith—should occur in our congregations as well as in our families. In addition, *we must affirm and encourage the development of one another's gifts*. How many husbands are concerned that their wives discover and utilize their gifts of the Holy Spirit and see their part in bringing this about? One of the major reasons God established the family was for the purpose of the mutual nourishing of our spiritual potential given by the Holy Spirit.

Yet how few of us who live together have struggled to develop this heightened potential within our relationships. Our homes have no disciplined atmosphere of Christian devotion. The joys of mutual prayer are often neglected. We actually compete for recognition, self-affirmation. We allow the weed of Me-First to choke our ground. Ministry, that miraculous

95

giving to one another of the Spirit of Christ, rarely soothes our battered psyches. We often must go outside our home if we are to find burden-bearers. As partners, we sometimes become draft horses pulling in opposite directions. Our straining influences the world little in terms of redemption. Married people need to come to terms with the many dichotomies which render their marital bonds a bondage; and many singles will have to overcome the idea that marriage is the only recognizable relationship in the world.

We do not start living when we get married. Marriage may never come to some. Moreover, it may not be the will of our Master for some lives. We can still establish relationships which contain the ingredients mentioned above. We can become family. We can duplicate the church within our rooms—minister first to one another, then as a team to the world beyond.

Some of the most effective ministers I know are single. Both professionals and lay single men and women have dramatically influenced me—those who have set themselves aside almost exclusively to the service of the Lord. We of Protestant background have scoffed too often at cloistered servants of God—those choosing to be single on the part of charity. Only Heaven will reveal the way the earth has been preserved unto His Coming through the prayers and good works of these fine people. We need to consider singleness as one choice for the purpose of ministry, rather than as a state attained by default. We need to recognize that it is a Scriptural option.

One of the most encouraging things for me to see as a pastor's wife is single people discovering their gifts and using their homes as places of ministry. When this happens I am aware that some barrier to growth has been crossed and a deeper maturation is taking place.

It is impossible to relate how often David and I have been uplifted by the unmarried people in our congregation. Two young women, for example, ministered to us with the gift of laughter. They made a point of celebrating Epiphany with us, each celebration growing more grandiose as the years passed. It began when they appeared on our porch on Twelfth Night, lantern and fruitcake and tambourine in hand, singing poignant carols. The next year was set aside with historical literary readings, dinner for four, and handmade gifts. Their combined sense of the ridiculous was healing. How often we gaily sat on their floor giggling and hee-hawing at the antics those two could contrive. After so much heavy counseling, it was good for nothing more to be required of us than our humor.

One ingredient singles living together don't have in common with marrieds (since even the possibility of children, foster or adopted, is open today) is the promise of a lifetime commitment; yet many have discovered that even temporal moments can be indelibly lasting when we make our own joyful memories.

Is love gone? Then we will pray for love and work to change the attitudes or circumstances which rob our life together of its joy. We will determine through communication, even that type which is painful, to develop welcome in our hearts toward each other.

If the welcome is gone, then we need to ascertain whether we take one another for granted, or if it is because deep-seated feelings of resentment have put down their bitter roots. In both cases honesty and forgiveness are essentials.

Sometimes taking one another for granted occurs simply because we are busy living separate lives. David suddenly realized after 12 years of marriage (I had stubbed my toe on this truth early, around year one of our union, nagged for a while, prayed next, reconciled the concern to God, actually forgotten about it until David reminded me of it) that we shared few extra interests beyond the common goals which joined us—that of the church and the children. Our hobbies and outside activities flew in scattered directions with mine winging toward the arts and nature and David's soaring in a steady course toward—the church. He has been accused of being single-minded (by me!).

We could foresee the potential difficulties this discrepancy might produce in the years ahead (when you remove children and church, what bonds are left?) and perhaps, even in the years present. Were we enjoying one another as much as we might? We chose several common interests—a sport, playing paddleball once a week at the Y; a literary interest, taking a course under a noted college professor on modern myth; a pragmatic occupation, gardening in our neglected back yard; and a purely pleasurable pursuit, studying drama including an annual excursion to Stratford, Ontario, Canada, for the superb Shakespeare Festival. Our hindsight has more than validated these efforts. Our life together has been greatly enriched. There has even been more confidence in the continued development of our independent pursuits. Since so much is shared, those activities we enjoy alone can only further enhance our life together.

Every relationship must undergo periods of evaluation. Is there as much new life between us as there was when we first met? Am I as intrigued by his/her interests? Are we learning from one another? (My foremost requirement of any friendship is that capacity to continue learning from each other.) If the answer to any of these questions is "no" then we must ask why and continue until solutions have been discovered. The most satisfactory unions are those which build, stimulate ideas, introduce me to worlds beyond my experience. People who share common thought patterns and personality traits offer definite soul-comfort and can lend great reinforcement by their understanding. But people who are different from ourselves can lead us into undreamed-of adventures.

Why is there no welcome in my heart? Is it because of self-centeredness? or resentment? because I have been betrayed? Deep work of the Spirit then has to be done. For most of us, however, it is a matter of simply developing new attitudes.

98

Let us work, then, on the welcome we extend to those with whom we live—not just the greeting given at the end of a long day, but the hospitality shared in the moment-by-moment meshing of lives. Let us demonstrate to one another, "Your ideas are welcome. Your interests are welcome. Your presence is welcome." Once we have opened these doors to each other we can begin to think about opening doors to the world outside.

Life Response

1. Check your welcome quotient. Are you glad to see those people with whom you live after a day apart? What is the tone of your usual greeting? Would you be happy if you received this response? If not, how can your manner be altered in order to convey welcome to your household companions?

2. What things would bring freshness to a living relationship that is growing a little stale? List them and then discuss them with your "family."

9

The Family of Joint-Heirs

FOR YEARS SOCIOLOGISTS AND ANTHROPOLOGISTS have devoted intensive study to that peculiar institution, the family. It has been examined in our society as well as in primitive cultures. The roles of husband and wife, mother and child, child and father have been systematically analyzed. The question is invariably asked, "How important is the family unit to the inward stability of a nation?"

At the beginning of this decade *Time* magazine culminated this investigation by running a feature article entitled, "The American Family: Future Uncertain." After developing its exposition on the demise of the family and the possible resulting negative influences on our culture, the writer devoted space to explaining the concept of the "nuclear family"—a unit containing one set of parents and their offspring.

This was contrasted to the family unit of earlier and less complicated days, the "extended family," where parents and their children were influenced by relatives who either lived in the same home or nearby. Here grandparents, great-grandparents, brothers, sisters, aunts, great-uncles, as well as a conglomerate gathering of their friends, lent great varieties of support—psychological, financial and emotional—to each other.

The nuclear family is a product of our mobile society where the average relocation occurs once in every three years. This new familial form is probably here to stay, but it will continue to endure great strain without the benefit of those important traditional supports. The husband and wife of today are forced to assume the total responsibility for what was once a group effort, and the pressures of these multiple roles are credited by the writer of the article as being partially the source for the high rates of divorce, alcoholism, and use of tranquilizers.

One authority on the family, psychologist Urie Bronfenbrenner, bemoans the segregation of age. He maintains that interaction with people of different ages is all-important to the preservation of the family. To end this segregation, which is particularly acute in suburban living, Bronfenbrenner and others recommend that architects plan community clusters where children, parents and the elderly can intermingle, each bringing experiences, knowledge and support to the other.

What an ideal opportunity the church has to provide an example of the extended family to a society bewailing its demise! Tom Skinner, the noted evangelist, speaks of the church as Christ's new community here on earth, a model to the world of what is happening in His kingdom in Heaven. Pointing to Acts 2 which reads, "And all the believers met together constantly and shared everything with each other, selling their possessions and dividing with those in need," he declares in his inimitable black style:

> We are a family. Brothers and sisters in Christ. What's mine is yours and what's yours is mine.
>
> Then when people ask, "Where's love?" we can answer, "Over here!"
>
> When they ask, "Where's justice?" we can answer, "Over here!"
>
> When they ask, "Where's unity?" we can shout, "Over here! In Christ's new community!"
>
> May I add that when they ask, "What's happened to the

family?'' we should be able to respond, "It's alive and
well. It's here—in *this* community cluster, this warm,
sheltering, loving, accepting body of Christ!''

True, many churches don't experience family—but they
can. A sense of life together can be developed. We are able to
create these opportunities within the body of Christ, among
the children of God, just as we can in our smaller household
groups—our families.

We need to first begin with the understanding that Christ
early in His ministry redefined family in terms of a larger inclu-
siveness. The record of this in Mark 3 (RSV) reads:

> And his mother and his brothers came; and standing out-
> side they sent to him and called him. And a crowd was
> sitting about him; and they said to him, "Your mother
> and your brothers are outside, asking for you." And he
> replied, "Who are my mother and my brothers?" And
> looking around on those who sat about him, he said,
> "Here are my mother and my brothers! Whoever does
> the will of God is my brother, and sister, and mother."

I don't believe Christ was demonstrating personal independence from a domineering mother and from relatives attempting to preempt His ministry, but rather He was laying the
groundwork for future understanding of relationships among
His followers. He was not teaching that we should exclude our
natural relatives, but rather that we should open our hearts to
those who share our common faith, to that "extended family"
of God.

In our modern churches the word "brother" is more an
affectionate address tagged onto someone's name than the in-
dication of a soul-bond which it was for the New Testament
writers. Romans 8:15-17 develops this doctrine of the brotherhood of the believers: ". . . but you have received the spirit of
sonship. When we cry, 'Abba, Father!' it is the Spirit himself

bearing witness with our spirit that we are children of God, and if children, then heirs, heirs of God and fellow heirs with Christ, provided we suffer with him in order that we may also be glorified with him" (RSV).

How then do we go about building "family" in our churches, becoming brothers and sisters in Christ in deed as well as name? *We can begin by getting to know one another.* We can start by talking with each other about our common faith.

In his book, *Full Circle,* my husband contends the basic reason the church forms is for this very fellowship:

> Conceivably, local churches could be eliminated were it not for the great need Christians have to discuss their faith with one another. An individual believer is able to worship or pray alone. He can share his faith apart from the church, and he can even adequately instruct himself along spiritual lines. It is obviously impossible, however, for him to participate in Christian fellowship without others who share his beliefs. I do not mean by this either to deprecate the value of corporate religious activities or to imply that interaction is the most important function of the church. Interaction is, however, that unique need which makes the formation of local church bodies mandatory.

Ironically, our very church structures, the buildings as well as the programs, inhibit this sharing of lives. Church pews are fastened securely to flooring, and admittedly, it is hard to talk to the back of a head. The majority of our meetings are dominated by lecture, and whereas we learn something about the lecturer, we come to know little about the man, woman or child sitting nearby. When unstructured events do occur, such as social evenings or baby showers, we are so unaccustomed to meaningful dialogue that we "fellowship" about everything but our faith—politics and baseball, children and recipes.

We have allowed the world to force us into its mold again.

We have assumed the masked charades of the culture around us, where innocence, candor and integrity are meaningless terms. We have learned to hide behind ego, the self we feel comfortable showing, not the self of the inner man. We have become powerless to tell one another who we are.

When Circle Church was started in the late '60s, one of the reasons for forming was to provide opportunities to meet this need for sharing around our common interest, the Christian faith. At 10:30, after the morning worship service, we gathered in various small discussion groups to talk about issues pertinent to our Christianity. Because we met in a Teamster's Union hall, the folding chairs aided us in forming many small groups all over the auditorium. Here we began the process of becoming comfortable in talking together about the things of our faith.

At first the Interaction Hour, as it was called, filled our need for fellowship. Seeing one another Sunday after Sunday in these small discussion groups helped us get to know the various personalities of our membership. As the church grew in size, however, the dialogue provided us with less opportunity for the personal understanding we desired. There then sprung into being small cells, meeting in homes for a variety of reasons. Some were Bible studies. Some formed for prayer. Others found methods to lend specific emotional and psychological support. The fact that we had no building of our own greatly aided these times of meaningful interaction, because we were forced to open our homes to one another. We were taking toddler steps toward family and discovering that hospitality, on many different levels, is one of the basic tools by which we learn to share lives.

The small group movement has enjoyed popularity among fellowship-starved churches over the last ten years. The home Bible study springs as much from a need for healthy interaction among Christians as it does from a concern for evangelism.

Church leaders must provide places within their programs to allow and encourage Christians to talk openly with one another about their common faith. The methods chosen to enhance this necessary interaction will be varied. Some may adopt the congregational form of sharing popularized by Ray Stedman's Peninsula Bible Church in California. Stedman's book, *Body Life,* describes these sharing meetings, where individuals in large churches stand to their feet expressing needs or testimonies of praise. Perhaps interaction will begin in programed Sunday school elective adult classes where one can choose from week to week which discussion would be most beneficial. Eventually, sharing, if it is to be most effective, will break into smaller units which meet regularly in the homes of the congregation members.

Generally, interaction takes its practice exercises on unthreatening turf, in academic discussions such as, "What is the meaning of eternal security?" or "How can we apply this understanding to our daily lives?" As we talk, we learn bits and pieces about how other group members think, and, if we are sensitive, we discover some of those hidden terrains where feelings dwell. Soon a comfortable trust factor builds, and often we are aided in expressing our inner thoughts by someone who is naturally more open. He can easily say "I'm really feeling lonely," or, "I've been having a terrific battle with depression."

Quickly true sharing begins to occur. Some grief or disappointment is too heavy to carry alone. It spills. Perhaps tears flow. We feel a little startled, a wee bit embarrassed; but again, one person seems to know how to express Christian love. It is done naturally, without ostentation, and teaches us all how beautifully these painful moments can be handled. The atmosphere in the room warms, and without knowing it we are on our way to more frequent experiences in sharing. One day we discover we are freely discussing not only the academics of our faith but the pragmatics—"How can I overcome this specific sin in my life?" "I can't seem to establish regular personal Bible study. Does anyone have any suggestions?"

In order to become a family we must learn to know one another. Once we know, we can love, for loving does not come unaccompanied by understanding.

A psychiatrist friend pointed out that perhaps even God's loving ability is increased by His capacity to understand His human creation. "When I am able to comprehend the inner workings of a disordered personality, it is often not until that moment that I discover empathy and compassion springing in my heart toward the patient," he explained. God is able to love us despite our actions because He knows from what past pain they tumble.

As Christians we can taste some of God's infinite understanding; but we must learn to talk to one another, to tell who we are, and why we are the way we are, and who we hope to become. Tolerance grows in our Body because we have had honest glimpses of those inner men. Sensitized through the work of the Holy Spirit, we become able to breathe deep draughts of compassion. Our hearts become opened to Him, and opened to one another, and His love is able to flow through us to our brothers.

Often we fear that if we identify our faults to our brethren, this information will be used against us. Generally, exactly the reverse occurs. When scientists were studying the habits of wolves, they noted an intriguing development. The researchers observed wolves fighting each other. When one clearly achieved dominance over the other, with hair and blood and passion raging, if the losing animal turned his throat and bared the jugular vein, the winning combatant would refrain from the death grip and allow his victim to go away, defeated, certainly, but alive. Something in that helpless appeal struck an instinctive chord of compassion in the beast.

So is it with us in this nonhostile environment of the church. I recall the extreme example of the pastor whose daughter revealed she was pregnant before marriage. With all intentions to marry, something had gone awry, and now the minister and his family and the young couple were on the horns of a dilemma. Putting the concern of his children before any personal considerations, he counseled that the two should come before the elders, confess their sin and ask for forgiveness. With tears and contrition, the act was done. The response was love, concern and support. The whirlwind of gossip was blown to sea with this difficult but courageous openness, and those two young people, having found release from guilt, were freed to advance together without detrimental bonds to the past. Today they serve the Lord excellently on the mission field.

Group leaders must put into practice this simple truth of sharing from weakness rather than from strength. Others will then respond in like measure and we will enjoy the marvelous climate of tolerance which eases itself into our congregations. We will come to understand that the loveliest gift we can give to each other is ourselves.

Recently some of the women at Circle Church have experienced a unique opportunity to share in small groups. A number of us happened to be together in discussion when we realized we all had expressed a common need to participate in intensive interaction with other women. We agreed to commit ourselves to one another over a two-month period, meeting in the quietest home once a week.

Establishing basic ground rules, we asked ourselves to: 1. Share as openly as possible; and 2. Pledge ourselves to become accountable to increase the spiritual disciplines of our personal lives.

"What shall we call this?" I wondered.

"Well, we've all stated we feel a need for spiritual growth," said one woman. "Why don't we call it a growth group."

Growth group it was indeed. We shared our lives as openly as possible. One was experiencing a battle royal with depression; another was entering into divorce; another was in the middle of divorce expecting a child and, for the moment, psychologically homeless. The other two of us had problems which were real, but nonetheless not quite so drastic. Needless to say, we had our hands full with each other.

Perhaps I had reached a point where my heart was simply hungry for deep relationships with other women, for these times of sharing satisfied something most inexplicable within me. In a survey of several hundred ministers' wives, David and I discovered that far and away the largest problem they faced was loneliness. When I shared this with my Catholic tennis partner, her reply prevented me from feeling sorry for women of my profession. She answered, "What? Them, too?"

Loneliness is a human condition. Each of us has to learn how to be a friend and how to make and keep friends. Due to isolation stemming from busy responsibilities and young children, I needed to cultivate friendship among those of my own sex. It was beautiful to "come home" each week to this small warm cell.

Over a period of two months we tasted each other's highs and lows. Because no time was taken in Bible study, we had several hours in which to enjoy the exploration of personalities. Often group Bible study becomes a substitute for personal pursuit of the Scriptures, and we sought rather to stimulate individual quests, to hold one another accountable for spiritual growth.

How often I have heard women state, "I need to be held accountable in this area (Bible reading, exercise, regular prayer habits, self-control of the tongue, etc.). Will you be responsible to hold me to development?" Knowing that next week someone would ask, "Did you spend time in Scripture?" or "Were you able to find time for prayer every day?" was great incentive to discipline. Often women wrote contractual agreements, pledging themselves to overcome their mutually difficult problem areas. If failure occurred, they would confess, ask for prayer, and begin once again.

Though emotional and psychological maturing were also handled, we felt these could be enhanced by an emphasis on personal Christian disciplines. We became convinced that the firm establishment of prayer and study and meditation were the basic fertile ground from which planted seeds could sprout.

The one small group mushroomed. Out of the first there was a woman who could lead another, and out of that perhaps two who were capable of shepherding others. Many asked to be a part of these small cells, indicating to me there were unfilled needs on the part of women in our local body. Within a year I had participated in five growth groups, and countless others have continued since, with the men of the church starting similar efforts of their own.

Certain patterns have emerged over these several years of growth-grouping. Within each there usually seems to be one or two individuals with heightened gifts of sensitivity. These know instinctively how to ask the right questions which open understanding in our minds. Each group usually contains some whose spiritual strength is a stimulus to the rest. Many groups have at least one emotionally fragmented person. All had one person I was sure I would never be able to love!

While I was assigning people to groups, I attempted to put together women with different needs and circumstances. There was always a mixture of single and married women; of the strong and, for the moment, of the not-so-strong; of the educated; of the creative; and of those convinced they were stodgy, uninteresting. Growth occurred as we learned from one another's different life situations. Singles heard of some of the agony of marriage; marrieds caught glimpses of the loneliness as well as the freedom of unmarried sisters. To our amazement we found that once sharing began, followed by increased understanding, there wasn't anyone we couldn't love. Indeed we were all lovable.

Closeness didn't come instantly, obviously. Generally the first four weeks were a time for getting to know one another on basic levels. Then I found it helpful to take a two-week break, after which we were eager to see one another and share again. The last four weeks were times of communion. Phone contacts throughout the week, ministries of mercy and kindness, purely enjoyable socialization began to burgeon. Our interaction on Sunday morning was more than, "Hi, how are you?" We had vital information to give to each other at this time. We had begun to truly bear each other's burdens. We were learning something of what it meant to be a part of the family of the joint-heirs of God.

Life Response

1. Find a small group. You may have to scavenge for a neighborhood Bible study, place a notice on the church bulletin board, or call together friends for intimate and regular prayer and sharing. Whatever the method, be sure not to deny yourself the rich pleasures of true spiritual fellowship with other Christians.

2. Find a small group *and become part of it*.

10

Open Homes

I AM CONVINCED THAT TRUE HOSPITALITY will only flower if our homes are open to each other. Hospitality enhances family. It is the responsibility of the church staff to provide opportunities for meaningful communication and growth within the programs and services. But it is the obligation of the laity to insure that substantial small group interaction occurs in living rooms, dining and kitchen areas, studios, and on front porches at the barest hint of spring. Back yards and basement recreation rooms, family boats, even cars can be places where we meet each other for this purpose of becoming family.

Many a pastor's wife participates in minimal efforts of hospitality because she realizes that, though she invites some, she may not be able to invite all. In fact, seminary courses in practical theology often stress this very attitude with what I believe are dreadful consequences. I'm convinced that if the staff aren't hospitable, the congregation won't be. David and I served in several situations where we weren't even invited to have coffee in the home of our senior pastor—and we were staff. Community in those churches seemed always to be budding, then dying on the vine. I vowed that if we ever had a church of our own, I would commit our home to establish a precedent of openness.

Yet I am not an idiot. I realize it *is* true—you can invite some, but you can't invite them all. When we were new and

113

few, David and I would bring the visitors of a Sunday morning service home for dinner. We never knew who would fellowship with us beforehand. The table was set for eight, the basic food preparations were completed, and we would load our valiant Volkswagen with whomever seemed not to have a place to eat. For years, every other Friday night we would invite 12 to 16 people for dinner. Through these efforts as well as frequent home-based church meetings, the regular attenders were often under our roof.

As we grew to a highly mobile congregation of several hundred, I realized it would be impossible to continue at this pace. It never entered my mind that I should consequently refrain from opening our private lives. The Lord was able to make me aware that my role was not to invite every one of 500, but rather to stimulate an atmosphere of hospitality, to demonstrate the expectation of hospitality being extended in all the homes of our people. The burden of "open homes—open lives," while it may be rooted in the attitude of the staff, must spread to the lives of the laity and continue to be tended by all.

When I look at hospitality as practiced in the Word I have a convicting sense of open homes—open lives, shared tables, ready comfort for weary travelers wandering on dangerous missions in their work for the Kingdom. The theme begins in the early records of the church, "And day by day, attending the temple together and *breaking bread in their homes*, they partook of food with glad and generous hearts, praising God and having favor with all the people" (Acts 2: 46, 47).

The home was integral to the early church. Formal worship for these Jewish Christians continued for many years to center traditionally in the Temple, but the home was the place where Christian fellowship occurred. "And every day in the temple and *at home* they did not cease preaching and teaching Jesus as the Christ" (Acts 5: 42).

The inclusion of Gentile believers and rejection by unsaved Jews brought the trend toward home churches. References in the New Testament abound. "To Philemon our beloved fellow worker and Apphia our sister and Archippus our fellow soldier, *and the church in your house* . . ." In Romans Paul sends greetings from his co-worker Gaius, *"who is host* to me and to the whole church"; in Colossians we hear of Nympha, "and the church *in her house"*; in I Corinthians we discover these phrases: "The churches of Asia send greetings. Aquila and Prisca, together with *the church in their house,* send you hearty greetings in the Lord. All the brethren send greetings."

In light of these and the others not recorded above, the injunction to "practice hospitality ungrudgingly" to one another makes reasonable sense. There were no building programs at this time. Church planting meant drawing together a group of people. In fact, the word "church" referred to a community of Christians. It did not indicate a structure.

No wonder Paul gives instructions that the elders were to be "given to hospitality." The New Testament body often congregated in their homes. I am not by this advocating that everyone must return to the home church. Nor am I saying that buildings are inherently evil. I am advocating that we shift our attitudes on hospitality into a clearer perspective and thereby realize the important role our homes play in establishing community and enhancing a feeling of family.

If the early church could weave a potentially fractious society of Jews and Gentiles, men and women, slaves and free into an interrelating harmonious community, so can we. We must demonstrate to society that peace, justice and brotherhood can exist in this world through the presence of Christ in a people.

When Christ sent out the 70 in twos, he taught them to expect hospitality in return for their Kingdom work—"Take no gold, nor silver, nor copper in your belts, no bag for your journey, nor two tunics, nor sandals, nor a staff; for the laborer deserves his food. And whatever town or village you enter, find out who is worthy in it, and stay with him until you depart" (Mt. 10:9-11).

115

He continues to give even greater meaning to open hospitality with these words from the same chapter, "He who receives you receives me, and he who receives me receives him who sent me. . . . And whoever gives to one of these little ones even a cup of cold water because he is a disciple, truly, I say to you, he shall not lose his reward."

The New Testament church obviously functioned according to their Lord's command. Allusions are sprinkled throughout to the hospitality they afforded one another. Paul, after his dramatic conversion, is harbored, vision-shocked and blind, in the house of Judas, a Damascus Christian. Acts 9 leaves record of Peter who "stayed in Joppa for many days with one Simon, a tanner." This same apostle jolts his Jewish brethren with his obedient openness and welcomes into his dwelling the Gentile messengers of Cornelius. They even spent the night, contrary to the ceremonial law of the Jews.

Delivered miraculously from prison, Peter goes to the house of Mary where many of the church were gathered praying for his release. After being beaten and imprisoned, Paul and Silas find refuge in the home of Lydia of Philippi.

Much of the apostles' ministry was centered in these private dwellings. Paul states, "how I did not shrink from declaring to you anything that was profitable, and teaching you in public and *from house to house*"; but the business of lodging these outspoken workers of the Kingdom was often fraught with dangers of its own. In Thessalonica a rabble crowd, incensed with the same apostle, "attacked the house of Jason, seeking to bring them out to the people. And when they could not find them, they dragged Jason and some of the brethren before the city authorities, crying, 'These men who have turned the world upside down have come here also, and Jason has received them; and they are all acting against the decrees of Caesar, saying that there is another king, Jesus.' " Security was taken from Jason and he was released, but his hospitality had been costly.

In Corinth, Paul shares the home of Priscilla and Aquila as well as going into their tent-making business in order to support his ministry. A poignant phrase included in this short narrative bespeaks ". . . lately come from Italy with his wife Priscilla, because Claudius had commanded all the Jews to leave Rome." Even in the face of dispersion they were able to share their lives with this one who had suffered so much for the Kingdom.

The documenting of hospitality continues—Philip the evangelist is credited with providing lodging to Paul as well as Mnason of Cyprus, "an early disciple." While journeying by ship under arrest, Julius the centurion treats the apostle kindly when they dock in Sidon and gives "him leave to go to his friends and be cared for."

Perhaps most notable of all is Paul's example as recorded in the closing verses of Acts. Not only a recipient, he practices what he preaches and at the first opportunity extends warm greeting in his own home. "And he lived there two whole years at his own expense, and welcomed all who came to him, preaching the kingdom of God and teaching about the Lord Jesus Christ quite openly and unhindered." The location? Rome. The occasion? Under house arrest, guarded by a Roman soldier, awaiting trial.

More than ever, society needs to see demonstrations of the meaning of family. Christ taught that those who do the work of God become part of the "extended family" of His Father. In order for this to happen, we must begin to share our lives. As we talk to each other honestly, we will achieve understanding, and love will not be far behind.

We must learn to think of the church as being without walls, and use our homes as tools of ministry. Once we have opened the doors, to our private selves as well as to our private dwellings, can the inheritance of this unique clan be slow in coming?

This has been a most difficult year in my life. Early last fall I was put to bed with a severe form of "over-ministry," a dis-

117

ease I have since discovered common to many a pastor and his wife. Nearly six months later, as I was beginning to feel strong again, my dear father became ill with an attack of encephalitis. We were informed several times during a week of crises to be prepared for his death. Though he lived, six months later he is still in a nursing home making infinitely slow progress with no guarantee of a return to normalcy.

Every few weeks seemed to harbor a disaster, great or small. Our three-year-old was hit by a fast-moving bicycle and was rushed to a hospital for twelve stitches uncomfortably near his eye. Our eldest lost a fingernail which got in the way of a pitched ball as he was attempting to bunt. We sustained two cases of scarlet fever, various throat and ear infections culminating in what seemed like weekly trips to the pediatrician. There were frequent visits to the community hospital 20 miles away to see my father, then to the rehabilitation center that was unable to rehabilitate, then to the nursing home with its wheelchairs and wandering senility and the 60-year-old mongoloid woman crying, "No! No! No!" for hours in the evenings.

The mechanical and physical supports in my life threatened to stop functioning. The washer stopped washing, the dryer stopped drying, the freezer couldn't decide whether to freeze, mushing my hand-picked cherries and wild blackberries and the summer's beans. The muffler went on the car. The kitchen faucet jammed and something under the sink pretended to be a fountain. The birthday Big Wheel lost a vital part which held the entire contraption together. Paint peeled on the eaves, and water leaked in the basement. One day I sat down and wrote four pages of complaints against God in my prayer notebook. Even the national economy seemed against us.

With Daddy sick I attempted to assume some of the responsibility for the retirement farm. It seemed suddenly important to plant the huge garden plot, nearly the length of two ranch-style houses. If health came again, if mentality was restored, life would be blowing in that fresh air, not the empty stares of dry-clodded earth or fruitless weed-riot. So we planted it willy-nilly one half morning and afternoon with children pounding tomato stakes and longing for the creek. The plants were too close together, and we lost the onions to wildness and the butternut squash got crowded out by the cucumber—I am only lately come to horticulture.

We angled the big tractor out of the barn and my 12-year-old son and I struggled with gears and chokes and levers in order to mow the huge lawn. We crawled on our knees to catch each good mulberry while the rest of last week's crop fermented on the ground under the huge spreading, nesting place.

One afternoon while pounding five-foot iron stakes with a 20-pound mallet in 93-degree heat in order to anchor the tender fruit trees with rubber hoses against the bending west wind, I noticed I was unusually tired. "It has been a long year," I thought, then hurried to finish a chapter in a book I was writing. I napped instead and woke feeling feverish. A blood test later revealed I had developed a case of mononucleosis, which lasts for six weeks—if you're lucky.

To bed again. I had endured work-stoppage that fall with grace. The illness of my father had tested my faith in the indomitable goodness of the Lord's will. I had looked on my mother's pain with hope for ease. The petty aggravation of broken things—equipment and bodies, had raised a slight spirit of anger; but this, this was the straw, and my spirit the camel's back. Days were spent on that pillow, head weighing a ton, fever stopping and starting, as I fought the despairing whys. I felt like a little child who had been spanked again and again for some unknown error. I was willing to change my unruly behavior but I didn't know what I was doing wrong.

One afternoon Mother came with food. The last thing she needed was to care for me. "Do you have this awful feeling that someone somewhere doesn't like us?" I ventured timidly, afraid to reveal my stricken feelings.

"No," she replied softly. "I have a feeling that Someone somewhere knows we won't be the people He wants us to be without pain. Don't ask where God's love is. This is His shadow side. It is here in these bad things." Laying her hands on me, she prayed for healing. My chastened soul found comfort and the wounds began to mend.

It is wonderful to find a natural mother who can give spiritual grace in the midst of her own trials. Yet, I discovered I was also part of a larger inheritance. For one year I was dependent on my joint-heirs in the Kingdom, on my "extended family" of God. They have turned to me hands of mercy and aid and helps.

> For I was weary, and they dusted and cleaned and scrubbed and laundered.

> For I was fatherless, and they helped me plant dry seeds of promise, symbols of resurrection—life springing from the dark underground. They tilled his soil with me in our helpless womanity, praying over the man-sized gas cultivator and stubbornly willing it to do a week's work in a day.

> For I was hungry, and they brought stews of the products of the good earth, and hand-kneaded breads still smelling of yeast, and apple pies from the fruit of the backyard trees.

> For I was imprisoned by the "manxome foe" despair, and they sat on my bed and wept as I wept, and brought guitars to concert me privately, singing, "If my head was like water and my eyes a fountain of tears, and I could mourn with the wounds of those who mourn."

> For I was aggrieved by the broken world, and they picked up my dropped baton and made the race with my battered friends for me. They sent prayers against the marred days and performed miracles over unwieldy faucets and the bent things that populated my heart.

> For I was helpless and they mothered my children, buy-

ing circus tickets and planning bike hikes, making sure the days were special for growing up.

For I was bereaved from bearing too much pain for others, finding no room for my own, and they sent me to restore in the mountains and rest in the sea.

Yea, as they did this all for me, they did it unto Him who sent me.

This is the larger part of my rich and goodly inheritance, this fellowship of suffering and delight, this place of belonging in a homeless world.

> Thank You, Lord, for these my brethren.
> Help us to always open doors to one
> another.

Life Response

Are the homes of the members of your church open or closed to one another? How would you rate the climate of community in your congregation? After these initial evaluations, find a pencil and paper. Sit quietly before the Lord and ask Him one question:

> "What role of hospitality would You have me play in helping to create a better feeling of family within my local church?"

Listen carefully, then begin to jot down any ideas which seem to drop into your mind. Don't lose your paper, but keep it as a list to remind you to be obedient.

11

The Finest House in Town

THE GREAT HOUSE WAS THE MOST BEAUTIFUL in town—not that it was so grand, but that it was so fine. Its sturdy foundation supported thick walls, expansive porches with turrets and buttresses tiptoeing skyward. Not one room was unfunctional, but each had been designed for a specific purpose. Each shingle and each tile of the roof was perfectly constructed, and the house's lathing and arch were cunningly crafted. Truly a Master Builder had been at work here.

Apart from the mortar and brick, the tile and stone, there was an unusual atmosphere surrounding the house, an excitement which said this was a household unlike any other. By night the windows shimmered with light, and by day, when the lanterns inside were dimmed, it seemed as though the lights were still shining. The people who lived in the house were also special. They shared and demonstrated such loving concern for each other, such caring. If one stood by the great gate, music and laughter could be heard coming from inside; and because it was a real house, an angry word might ever so often pierce the atmosphere, but never haranguing or violent ranting.

Even the life growing outside, the shrubbery and flowering bushes, the bending trees, the budding plants seemed finer than the other gardens in town, more content to be about the business of growing. The same storms beat upon these grasses and plants, the same winds blew and tore, the same harsh summer sun burned as on the other gardens in town, but any damage was cleverly turned to advantage by the gardener who did his pruning with a careful knife and a firm but gentle hand.

Evalyn All was not from such a fine house. She lived in one of the shanties which crowded upon the backwaters. A small wood-burning stove heated the hut in winter—if there was wood—and water was drawn from the brakish stream outside, the conduit for the disposals of the towns and factories up-river. Evalyn lived with her older sister and three younger brothers and a mother who disappeared for days, then reappeared without warning.

In her yearning for a better life, Evalyn All would go and watch the fabric of life woven daily around the great house. She would hide behind a bush near the gate and watch and watch, her big eyes observing even the tiniest details. She noted that the clothes of the people were always clean. In summer they dressed in white. The piques and dotted swisses and organdies of the little girls shone brightly in the sunshine and Evalyn wondered—*How do they keep their things so clean?*

One day a small boy fell on the gravelway. From her hiding place, Evalyn saw the gardener turn, gently wipe away tears, prepare a herbal salve, then bind the bloodied knee. She turned her back to the fence. The longing beating in her soul was too much to bear.

As the seasons changed, the foliage on the hiding bush fell to the ground. Suddenly Evalyn All discovered that she could be seen by the occupants of the great house and that none of them seemed to mind her presence. When one man smiled cordially and nodded his head in greeting, she took heart and walked to the very gate itself. Since there was no necessity to hide, she mustered enough boldness to walk completely around the iron fence.

The kitchen was in the rear, and if Evalyn All stood by the

fence there, she could smell bread baking, its yeasty aroma saturating the air. It filled her nose and lungs and triggered a hungry ache in her empty stomach.

A marvelous fountain bubbled beside the back porch, and she was to discover that even in the coldest of winter it flowed, and frost scarcely iced its edges. Evalyn imagined how wonderful such clear and sparkling water would taste on the tongue, how it would roll over the palate, how its freshness might linger even after being swallowed.

As the days grew colder, the people in the great house exchanged their summer whites for garments of scarlet, warm flowing robes that protected them from winter chills. Evalyn All shivered through her daily pilgrimages. If she could just have one small taste of that fresh bread—

For days Evalyn All was ill. She burned with fever and often cried out something her brothers and sisters couldn't understand, "Please, please let me come in! I'll be so careful. Please let me come in." It was several weeks before she was strong enough to return to the gate by the great house, the finest one in town. She slipped out at night, while her sister was sleeping.

She had never seen the house so beautiful. A fresh snow frosted the cornices and eaves and spread a blanketed shimmer over the garden. The lights of the house shone and glistened in reflection on the winter white. Fires crackled in the fireplaces. The massive front doors were flung wide and men and women walked to and fro, their warm scarlet cloaks protecting them from the cold air. Evidently, the house had been prepared for a great celebration. Evalyn could see garlands festooning the receiving rooms, and bright flags lining the driveway where highly polished carriages traversed, unloading their elegantly attired owners.

Suddenly light-headed, she sank down on a stone and rested her forehead in her hands. The lights in the house blurred and she felt weak.

"You'll be all right," said a voice. Startled, Evalyn All

looked into the face of an old man, gnarled and misshapen. "Felt the same way myself, lotsa times. Cold and hungry and too tired to feel a blasted—" He stopped angrily in mid-sentence.

"Do you live—" Evalyn All started, but before the question was finished she knew it was impossible. The man wore clothes like hers, old and dirty. "O nuh," came the answer before she could finish. "Nuh, nuh, nuh. There was a time when I hoped, too . . ." and he sighed. "But I'm past hoping. Got useta and like the way I live. Y'gotta have an invitation, y'know." Evalyn's heart sank, because she'd been hoping too.

"Yessir . . . gotta getcha an in-vi-ta-tion. Them's the rules." They sat in silence, the melody from the house floating around them, creating longing for dancing, for joy. "Yup, useta come here every day when I'se a little guy. Useta watch and wait and hope somebody'd say—'Whydoncha come in.' But it never happened. Don't come anymore, don't even wanna see the place 'cept once in a while, like tonight, for the celebration. But them, the wretches, they haven't lost hope."

"Them?" said Evalyn All. "Who do you mean?"

"Why, them!" shouted the old man. "Them, them, them!" He threw his hand toward the shadows and shades of the darkness. Evalyn peered, her eyes squinting, but she could see nothing in the night. "Come on! I'll show them to ya," he cried and impatiently grabbed her arm, dragging her after him.

Evalyn All stumbled in the blackness. The old man was rough, not careful to protect her as they rushed to the back of the house. The smell of baking bread began to reach her, her knees buckled, but her companion was relentless in his pursuit. "Them! Them!" he screamed and pointed. "Them's the ones that's hungry!" Suddenly, Evalyn All could see. Standing by the iron fence was a group of people, emaciated, starving skin barely stretching over bone. They drooled at the mouth and sniffed at the air as though smelling enough would fill their hollows inside.

126

The old man grabbed her arm again and they stumbled to another place in the fence. "Them! Them! Them what's sad!" Evalyn All could see. Hanging on the fence were people with tears streaming down their cheeks. They pushed and shoved trying to get closer to hear the music which seemed to be clearer on this side of the house, like a bell. Oh, how it lifted the heart! If only she could hear it better, but the old man had again clutched at her.

"Them! Them!" he chortled, a shriek rising in his throat. "Look and laugh!" Evalyn All looked. Every inch of the fence was crowded by people. She had never seen anything so mournful in all her life. Nearby a small boy pressed his face between the bars of the iron gate, his tiny fists gripping tightly. "What's your name?" asked Evalyn All, but there was no reply. The boy turned his face to her and, in the glow from the house, she could see that he was blind. "Got no tongue neither," came the grave voice of her guide. "Been mistreated. Happens all the time."

"Fools!" the old man spat out. His voice narrowed and he whined, "Waiting for an invitation, they are. Never gonna get one." The narrowness of his voice flattened, widening into indisputable hatred. "Not supposed to be this way. Supposed to invite us in. Supposed to come find us."

"Who?" asked Evalyn All, numbed by her revelation of misery.

"Those what's in the house, *but they don't even know we're here.*"

Evalyn shuddered. How could they not see—how could SHE not see— "Jest too busy in their own house to look. WHYDONCHA LOOK!!" he screamed. "Whydoncha look . . . whydoncha?"

Remembering Evalyn All, he took her hand again and pushed her closer to the iron fence. "Over there. Can you read?" and he pointed to the cornerstone. She shook her head; she had never learned. "Maybe it's jest as well," said the wizened guide. "Gots the founder's name chiseled in the stone. Celebratin' for him tonight—"

Evalyn All looked at the people standing in the dark shadows of the night. Their faces were turned toward the light. Their silence was overwhelming. She heard a baby cry. "Abandoned," mumbled the old man to himself. "Yup, 't happens sometimes."

Evalyn turned her back and walked away from the light and the music and the aroma of fresh, warm, yeasty bread. She turned from the crackling fireplaces and the bubbling fountain and the laughter and the scarlet garments and went back home, back home, back to the shack by the river. It was many, many years before Evalyn All walked again past the gate of the great house, the most beautiful house in town. When she did, she didn't even turn her head.

Why are our efforts at evangelism often abortive? Because the church has lost the awareness that it is a household of God into which we are to invite the weary and downtrodden, in spirit as well as in body. Somewhere in the history of the American church—perhaps because of our growing affluence which made it possible "to do it by ourselves," certainly in response to the Western democratic emphasis on autonomy and personal independence—the sense of community was lost to believers. When this concept of "shared lives" became a mystery to us, we began to exist as individuals with arbitrary commitments to a body of believers.

The church has little experiential knowledge of that beautiful household described in Ephesians 2:17 (RSV):

> And he came and preached peace to you who were far off and peace to those who were near; for through him we both have access in one Spirit to the Father. So then you are no longer strangers and sojourners, but you are fellow citizens with the saints and members of the household of God, built upon the foundation of the apostles and

prophets, Christ Jesus himself being the cornerstone, in whom the whole structure is joined together and grows into a holy temple in the Lord; in whom you also are built into it for a dwelling place of God in the Spirit.

Not only are the iron gates closed to those standing in the darkness waiting for an invitation, but we have barricaded our lives from one another. The daily efforts—gardening, picking beans, spraying bugs, tending broken knees—as well as the celebration of God's indwelling Spirit—are lost to us. We no longer know how to coexist in the seasons of one another's lives.

Consequently, newborn babes often starve if they can't find a spiritual household with an open door and provision of the sweet warm milk and protein-rich meat of the Word. Slightly muddled, not sure what we are about, we allow the infant to fend for itself. Our house stands; it is there for all to see. It has been crafted in perfect intent by the Master Builder, but all too often the spirit of those within is feeble. Those who abide in these nearly emptied edifices can scarcely hear the cries of strangers beyond the gates.

Unfortunately, the efficiency of those "arms of the church," the almost technological efforts of mass evangelism, have progressed far beyond the development of the "householding" of God. Often the results have been tragic. Children brought into any world, whether it be of this earth or of the spirit, will die if they are not nurtured in a loving home. It matters not where the fault lies. Too many evangelism efforts have remained unconcerned about their offspring, and too many churches have not experienced family to the degree that they were able to take care of their own offspring, let alone assume the responsibility for someone else's child. Evangelism without a functioning household of God will result in a high mortality rate.

Several years ago someone said to my husband that if the

church continued in the lifeless pattern it had established, it would be all but dead in ten years. This was obviously an overstatement, but the Lord used those words to jog David. He resolved if that was true, he would dedicate his life to bringing renewal in some way to the church. All our friends at the time were involved in evangelistic efforts and most strongly advised that the church was not the place "where the action was." Despite this negative encouragement, David determined to steer our little family to serve in the church, and the inner-city, from which many Evangelicals had fled.

It has been our privilege to share almost every breathing moment with an intense, eager brotherhood who are dedicated to experiencing life within the church. Truthfully, we have fluctuated between tasting the defeat of "paradise lost" and the excitement of "paradise regained." I will not pretend that being a part of any household can be an easy or instantaneous success.

We have also taken our assigned place beside a dedicated minority who for 20 years have applied patience, creative ability and creativity to the problems of the traditional church which are only now beginning to reap results. It has been amazing to struggle locally with some lesson the Lord is teaching us only to discover that He is calling other test-tube congregations on a national level, though scattered geographically, without prior mutual communication, to the identical tutelage. We are convinced because of the direct input on a grassroots level, as well as a comprehension of God's Spirit blowing on a broader worldwide community, that windows are being thrown open, rooms aired, fires lit on the stone hearths, dry fountains plumbed, food stocked in empty kitchens, the front doors flung wide, gardens tended, people welcomed.

Each renovation makes place for the Spirit of Life to build also into human efforts, to tabernacle in this once locked room, in this formerly dusty attic. Christians are growing into an organic temple. They are not satisfied any longer with being an inn for transient wayfarers who are mainly concerned about the business of their other world. Once "household" has been reestablished locally, we will be able to make room for long-lasting mass evangelism efforts. We may even be able to reassume that task, this midwifery of the spirit, as one of the primary functions of the church.

Life Response

Close your eyes and imagine that shining household described in this chapter. Imagine those starving, freezing, defeated people waiting for an invitation. Ask the Lord to open the eyes of your soul to help you see the real people of your community who are longing to come in.

12

Householding

IN THE SUMMER OF 1974 the International Congress on World Evangelism was held in Lausanne, Switzerland. Amazingly, the coordinators were able to divide 10,000 believers representing 156 countries, meeting over a period of nine days, into small groups in order to develop a strategy for evangelism. These divisions were concerned with four basic thrusts which included: 1) *National strategy groups* where the participants from a particular country met every day to answer two basic questions: How can we best complete the evangelization of our own country? What unique contributions does our nation have to make to world evangelization at this point in history? 2) *Demonstration of evangelistic activity groups*. 3) *Strategy of evangelization study groups*. 4) *Theology of evangelization study groups*.

The facts derived from this convergence of believers were several. The church is growing proportionally faster than the population in many parts of the world, such as Brazil, East Africa and India. There are now more than 200 non-Caucasian, non-European, non-Western foreign missionary societies. There are still 2.7 billion people who have not heard the Gospel.

The results of this convocation have been multiple—certain individual countries have been galvanized into activity. Perhaps just as important, the Lausanne Congress has reminded many that the household of God holds global implications. Christians need to recall while participating in local efforts of soulwinning, when giving verbal witness to a stranger on a train, when meeting in a small Bible study, that the pilings upon which the foundations of this building have been poured are sunk deeply into the four corners of this planet. Flickering in the provincial capital of a tiny mideastern country 2,000 years ago, this faith has flamed in the face of war, treachery, famine, disaster. Sometimes the light has sparked from candle to candle, then burned forlornly alone in dark places; at other times it has swept in as revival fires. Evangelism has always been part of God's worldwide strategy. We are inviting people to experience not only changed lives, but shared lives.

God is creating His household on the face of this spinning planet. Through Jesus Christ He is redeeming this world to its original design. One day when our Lord comes again in glory, man will be restored to what he was primarily intended to be. He will be like that man/God who was earthbound temporarily but who fleshed out for all history to understand what truly was the Creator's original intent. Man will be filled again with the Spirit of God.

Society will harmonize. War and injustice will give way to the law and order established by a just Judge and a benevolent King. Man will be able to live in peace with man. There will be no disadvantaged, oppressed or underprivileged.

Throughout our marriage I have been privileged to watch firsthand the workings of personal evangelism due to David's facility. It first became apparent when we were newly married and involved in the work of Youth for Christ. It seemed as though every week some teen was led to a new relationship with Jesus. In fact many of those people are a part of our church ministry at present. It's a thrill to have someone say, "Don't you remember? You led me to the Lord when I was in high school."

As this pattern continued, I concluded that David obviously

had something I didn't have. I knew all the words, could explain all the terms, could find the Scripture references—I even memorized my husband's pattern—but it was he who led people to Christ, not me. This is not to say that I was inarticulate about my faith. People who know me will testify to the fact that it is impossible for me to be nonverbal about anything! In fact my neighbors have been known to accuse me of steering conversation. "We're talking about religion again. Karen must be here!" Yet I seemed to lack some instinct, some comprehension of timing endowed to David whereby he sensed the inner longing of the heart. He knows when to draw the net and when to cast it out and when not to take the trouble to go fishing at all.

Early in the beginning of the Circle Church ministry we began to discover in Scripture the teachings concerning the gifts of the Holy Spirit. This freed me from a guilty bondage, particularly those words from Ephesians 4:11, 12: "And his gifts were that some should be apostles, some prophets, some evangelists, some pastors and teachers, to equip the saints for the work of ministry, for building up the body of Christ. . . ." David did have something I didn't have! He had an active gift of the Holy Spirit.

Further freedom came when I realized that every Christian was gifted and responsible before God for the development and use of his own gifts. For years I had been trying to do something I wasn't equipped to do. From this point in understanding I set about to work on the abilities I knew the Holy Spirit had given me, one of which was the gift of hospitality.

Once we began to open our home for the purposes of ministry, I discovered that my facility became linked with David's gift of evangelism. We soon began to function as a team, working hand in glove. I can't count the times when, with the room softened by candleglow and our hearts by the Spirit, our conversation has lingered into the wee hours with someone finally bowing head and heart before his Savior.

135

Our mutual gifts were bathed in prayer—David's that the Lord would make ready hearts, mine that He would make a ready home, and then that He would cover us with that supernatural sensitivity to timing and intent. We fully realized we were dependent upon Him to create from the evening something more than the enjoyment of food and ideas. It is humanly impossible to stimulate an atmosphere where spirit-work is done apart from the Spirit. The miracle of conversion has happened so often through our joint efforts that our house is something like a spiritual maternity ward. David is the obstetrician in charge, to be sure; but I am a nurse in the labor room.

One particular example of all this stands out in my memory. Very often David will lead an after-service class which deals with the topic, "What does it mean to be a Christian?" Three couples attended one session where the wives were all believers and the husbands were not. Due to their interest and the lack of time, we invited these to dinner for the express purpose of examining further the meaning of Christianity.

The rooms seemed to have a special glow that night—perhaps we were surrounded by the unseen presence of Christ. At any rate, after due deliberation one young man bowed his head and invited the Lord to make a place within his inner self. Lifting his head after the prayer he asked for a drink of water. While filling the glass it was my privilege as hostess to remind him of those words of Jesus, "If any one thirst; let him come to me and drink. He who believes in me, as the Scripture has said, 'Out of his heart shall flow rivers of living water.' "

Then David turned to one other young man and asked, "Mike, how close do you think you are to making the same decision?" His wife replied with gentle humor, "Well, he hasn't come to term yet, but the labor pains are about three minutes apart." Eventually all came to know the Lord.

Hospitality is not the only gift which can enhance evangelism. Sometimes conversion cannot come until other loving ministries have been applied. If there is emotional fragmentation, counseling skills involving wisdom or knowledge or discernment may need to be invited. If there is hunger, mercy may need to be shown. If there is distress, aid may need to be given. These gifts till the soil, fertilize the ground, and prepare for the evangelist who knows how to harvest the field to insure the maximum yield. It is the household, however, which knows how to guarantee minimum spoilage. The gifts are one of the reasons I feel strongly that evangelism should not be separated from the functioning of the church.

By no means am I minimizing evangelism. But I am attempting to emphasize what I feel has been greatly neglected, the fact that according to Scripture we are not all evangelists. We have been gifted differently. We need to understand that through the development of these supernaturally endowed abilities we can greatly aid in the process of spiritual birth as well as creating a trusting family in the church.

Perhaps it would be wise to insert here that we are also taught to pray for the higher gifts, and I believe the Lord is now asking me to devote myself to request this. There is a spring of bubbling water growing within me, and from this I can give draughts to those thirsty people standing beyond the iron gates.

Each of us can participate in some way in evangelism through hospitality—the use of the home as a tool of ministry. The genius of the home is that it is universal to each Christian. We all abide somewhere—in a room or a dormitory or an apartment or a bungalow. In this inhospitable world a Christian home is a miracle to be shared. Perhaps a child needs shelter from her mother's shrieks by resting on our stairs. Maybe someone will knock on our door with tears in her eyes looking for peace. There's not one of us who can't say, "Come in. Why don't you come in?"

If we understand that we are stewards to a divine Master, we must consider why we are in this place at this time in this town. He is not haphazard in His planning. Someone in this block weeps behind closed doors—someone is crying. Loneliness stalks the halls of this high rise; bad news has been posted somewhere in this nearby community.

The Lord has recently convicted me of my insensitivity toward the problems and pains of my neighbors. There have been hospitalizations and distress—a multitude of opportunities to extend love—but I was prevented by the lack of time and even financial resources. Yet I know He orders my days, and I am committing to Him the minutes thereof, asking that He will enable me to reach out to these friends in their need, to demonstrate the reality of my Christianity. At night before I fall asleep I begin to pray for each house on the block, asking that the peace of God will reach out to each dwelling, praying that the inhabitants will begin to search for happiness, and hunger after righteousness. I commend to each the love of Christ and request that He will enable me to be an instrument of that love. If I fall asleep midway, I pick up the next night where I left off the evening before, so that the whole neighborhood will be covered by my prayers.

Unfortunately, insensitivity is not just my problem; it is often the major fault of the church. We become ingrown. If we are not what Christ expects us to be, we have nothing to share; and if our household is filled with His presence, we often become so enamored with the fellowship and activities of this warm brotherhood that we forget to look for those hanging on the fence, or spying on us from a hiding bush, or waiting for an invitation.

Sensitivity will come as we labor in prayer. In fact, if the work of evangelism is not first instigated in prayerful conduct, that's a pretty fair sign it will have only human results. We may even keep people from knowing Christ by our blundering dogmatism and judgmental attitudes toward a different life-style. Without prayer we begin to get nervous about winning people to Christ, we think we can relate the number of scalps collected to the depth of our spirituality, we become insistent, pushy, offensive. Soul work is always God's work. We are simply instruments through which He can channel Himself. Going to Him on our knees is the discipline by which we become effective evangelists.

Having lived in six different communities during our married life, I have never felt lonely around my neighbors. We have dwelt in the homogeneous suburbs, in the convulsive inner city with its great ethnic variety (which everyone, by the way, warned would be cold, and which I found delightfully neighborly); and now in a town on the verge of racial change. In every place we have extended invitations to landlords and shopkeepers, barbers and janitors, women, men and children. I've had luncheons and teas and coffee breaks, birthday parties and pancake breakfasts and just plain old chatting over the fences. I am not lonely, because I refuse to be alone, and I have *never* met anyone who was offended because I opened my door and invited her (or him) to come in.

The home of the Christian is a tool for ministry. Ask the Lord how He wants you to use it. He may speak to your ear that He wants you to start Bible studies. One woman I know of heard just this very thing. "All right," she replied. "I'll go up and down the block knocking on each door, *but You are responsible for the results*. If no one comes, that's not my concern, but Yours." Many did come, and that one Bible study has had tremendous results.

The Lord may ask each of us to use our homes in a different way. Once we are obedient, having bathed the rooms in prayer, we can sit back and let the Lord do His own work. There will be no need for manipulation or contrivance. I've had people come into our home with so much curiosity about the work of the church, and the particular beliefs we hold on the faith, that we have, for courtesy's sake, had to declare, "Now we've talked about ourselves enough. You tell us about your life." The results are His. We must be faithful with the use of the tools.

139

The phone rang some days ago with a message in which we rejoiced. Sandy had led her neighbor Marilyn to the Lord. This story begins over a year ago when Sandy and Jim bought a home. It was a sad little house (with possibilities), forlornly neglected by the eccentric old man who had lived there for years and years. Yet it was a bargain if the labor could be provided free of charge. Another of our church members lived on the same block, and she organized work forces which for two weeks scrubbed and painted and scraped and pounded. Once all this was completed, moving crews carried furniture and boxes and bags into the house, which was definitely a lot happier looking now. It was an example of how we are learning to share lives in our congregation.

Sandy and Jim have many abilities, one of which is a heart for evangelism as well as an open door. Being spiritually mature, they began their work in prayer, asking the Lord to show them the reasons why they were living in that house, on that block, in that town. They began to take advantage of opportunities to meet their neighbors. And they began to initiate relationships. They created hospitable situations—evenings for dinner, sharing birthday parties, attending social functions with neighbors. A Bible study was started and many invited. Through all this they established special communication with one couple in particular—the wife proclaimed herself to be an atheist. The dialogue between them began to center more and more around spiritual things with no rushing on Sandy and Jim's part, but much prayer which was also borne by others in our household of faith.

One fall evening the women were canning applesauce together and they began to discuss the meaning of being a Christian, the difference this made in one's life. "I didn't feel a freedom to press the issue," explained Sandy. Considering that the clock was creeping toward midnight and they were surrounded by hot-water baths and steaming jars, this was probably wise. But in the next couple of days the same conversation resumed, and at this time, in obedience to the prompting of the Holy Spirit, Sandy asked if Marilyn might not like to commit herself to Christ. The response was "yes."

"You know," confided Marilyn. "When I saw all those people from your church working on the house and moving you in, I knew you all had something I didn't have. And when I told you I was an atheist and you didn't get upset but just listened and tried to answer my questions without imposing what you believed on me, I was sure of it."

I love this story—because of its happy ending, to be sure— but also because it illustrates many of the things in which I believe strongly. If the household of God is real, people will want to be a part of it: "By this shall they know you are my disciples, in that you love one another." And if we learn to open our homes and our lives, we can draw to Him those who live across the hall, or who share our parking spot, or who own the farm across the pasture, or who check out groceries at the store. We can learn to employ all the common incidents of living for His favor—"Can you come help me eat the pie left over from dessert?" "Let's can applesauce together." "Darryl has extra tickets to the ball game. Can you and the kids come?" "We just bought a pool table. How 'bout a game?"

Then at night we can think about those who are in the darkness, hungry for bread and thirsty for water, longing for crimson robes and glistening garments, searching for a song, waiting at the gates. We can pray that He will help us to hear their cries, to see their longing, to invite them to come into our rooms, our lives, our wonderful and fine and beautiful household of faith.

Life Response

1. Try my prayer exercise for falling asleep. Each night begin to pray for the people who live around you. Pray up

and down the block, through your unit of apartment buildings or the individual rooms in the dormitory. Start the next night where you left off the night before.

2. Record in a notebook the ways the Lord answers your prayers. This method is a good way to sensitize ourselves to the fact that He is truly working in our lives.

13

Open Hearts

TERESA OF INDIA, who founded the Society of the Missionaries of Charity in 1950, rises at 4:30 each morning in order to be ready with her fellow sisters to work in the streets and sidewalks of Calcutta with "the poorest of the poor." Born in Yugoslavia in 1910, this unusual woman had been in India for 17 years and was principal of a Loreto convent school when, on a train to Darjeeling for a retreat in 1946, she "heard the call to give up all and follow Him into the slums to serve."

Taking vows of extreme voluntary poverty, she began her work among the displaced of society, the outcasts of outcasts. In caring for the leprous, the orphaned, and those filled with disgusting disease, she serves as unto Christ. She and her co-workers choose to see Him in the eyes of the maimed beggars. The love they give to those awaiting death in the streets is the love they would give as unto their dying Lord.

In 25 years the Society has grown into a worldwide organization, with 954 sisters operating 80 homes for the poor—26 of them outside India, in such places as Peru, Tanzania, and even New York's South Bronx. "Our work is for people who have forgotten how to smile, forgotten the human touch and have a greater hunger for these than for a plate of rice. Such hunger is even greater in the West than in India and Africa, where the problem is material poverty."

World attention was focused on Mother Teresa a decade ago

through a televised interview conducted by the English news commentator, Malcolm Muggeridge. So impressive was her work that he traveled to India with a photographic team in order to document her unusual life-style on film. The experience of this venture is recorded in his book *Something Beautiful for God*.

In it he recalls his strange experience in the Home for the Dying, a shelter established as a hostel of peace and love where sickly, abandoned people from the streets could die in dignity. The cinematographer was certain that nothing would be captured on film because the natural light in the building was so dim. Disappointed, the team shot pictures anyway. When they received the prints they were amazed to find that an unusual illumination made the scenes visible. Muggeridge concludes that it was the light of the presence of something supernatural, an incandescence beyond the seeing eye, something to do with the utter calm which surrounded the rooms in which these people lay dying.

The life of this woman who is revered in India as the Saint of the Sidewalks illustrates the type of radical hospitality the church is guilty of neglecting. We have turned our backs on the poor and powerless of the world, allowing them to die in their sufferings, abdicating our responsibility to institutions. I always wonder what the size of the welfare rolls would be if the evangelical church had not neglected her social concern. Has our land lost its flavor because we so callously refused to salt its cities and ghettos with Christlike concern?

The Lord began His ministry by proclaiming a standard I believe is suitable for us all: "The Spirit of the Lord is upon me, because he has anointed me to preach good news to the poor. He has sent me to proclaim release to the captives and recovering of sight to the blind, to set at liberty those who are oppressed, to proclaim the acceptable year of the Lord" (Lk. 4:18, 19, RSV).

Christ came to all men, but His message of redemption

found particular appeal on the part of those disenfranchised, without hope, under the heel of unrighteous oppressors. We dare not neglect those who are abandoned by their fellow humans. For the Christian there is no caste, no race, no sex discrimination. We must minister to all people.

While driving to a speaking engagement, I questioned a companion about her job as a state social worker. Her particular function was to find placements for foster children. Did she feel a sense of fulfillment despite the frustrations, I wondered? "Yes," she replied. "Particularly in cases like Timmy Miller's."

It seems as though Timmy had spent the major portion of his eight-year-old life chained by his grandmother to a radiator in his room. Food was brought to him and he was allowed to defecate and urinate on newspapers. There were other children in his family who were not treated similarly. For some warped reason Timmy had been singled out.

When Timmy's condition finally reached the attention of officials, it fell to my friend Mary to find a home for him. Would you be able to share your home with a child who had existed like an animal most of his life? Someone could. A pastor with 11 children, some natural, some adopted, some under foster care, amazingly found room in his heart for this oppressed boy.

"Do you know," marveled my friend as we continued to travel. "We are discovering that Timmy has a 'gifted intelligence quotient.' The only fortunate thing about his story is that, although confined, he could see and hear the television set, which was on constantly."

In my unconscious moments before I fall into deep sleep, I frequently imagine children like Timmy—the world's children—stomachs bloated, eyes resigned to suffering, bodies and spirits abused, battered and maligned. I am jolted awake, and often in a cold sweat, with heart beating wildly, I send out prayers against such agony.

For years I have said to the Lord, "Father, if you want me to take into our home one of these disadvantaged children, please bring that child to me. By this I will know it is Your will." One day He did, but that child was 26 years old. She had experienced two years of mental hospitalization, six months of it in a catatonic condition. Haunted by shock treatment, she was suffering from memories of her existence in a state institution. We realized this "child" the Lord had brought into our lives would never be able to know God's love until she had experienced a loving Christian family.

From firsthand experience David and I know the painful despair and joyous delight of what I call "radical hospitality"—taking people with need into one's own home. We learned tremendous lessons, had our strength utterly spent, found the compensations sometimes remarkable, sometimes nonexistent.

Another way the Lord has answered this prayer is by allowing me to serve on the board of the Evangelical Child and Family Agency, an organization which began 25 years ago when an infant was abandoned in a cardboard box at the door of the Moody Bible Institute in Chicago. The inference was clear that the mother wanted her child to be reared in a Protestant home; but there was no specific agency to provide placement service for Protestants.

Clearly a need existed, and a group of ministers and lay people began this agency, which has stimulated much concern over its one-quarter century of existence. ECFA now provides adoptive services, placing "children with special needs"; it coordinates foster family care, conducts an unmarried parent program, and provides family counseling.

For years I have wondered if Christians could make a substantive difference in our society by concentrating on giving shelter to these rejected children. What would happen if each Evangelical church would call out three to five gifted couples to consider the ministry of foster-family care?

What would happen if the congregations would rally—if doctors would volunteer free medical aid for those hard-to-place children with physical problems; if Christian therapists and psychologists would pledge themselves to help with emotional disorders—what would happen? What could we accomplish for the cause of Christ in metropolitan Chicago if families in churches opened their doors? What could occur in farming communities if people opened their hearts? What results are possible across the nation if we become faithful in just this one small area of social concern?

I am far from inferring that everyone has the ability to be hospitable to a needy child. In fact, I believe just the opposite—few of us have such highly developed gifts of hospitality that we can exercise them in these radical ways. There are few who can bear the pain these types of commitments require. Nevertheless, I believe we lack vision in our outlook. *There are many more qualified by the Holy Spirit to do this type of work in the world than are doing it now.* Some of us may be sinning because of our nearsighted neglect.

Jimmy showed up at the Chicago Police Department. He wondered if they could find him a place to live. It seems as though Jimmy's only parent was alcoholic and things had become unbearable at home. A call was placed to ECFA who in turn began to make calls of their own. One couple contacted already had a foster child plus several natural children, and the wife explained the impossibility of caring for any more.

She related the call to her husband and assured him she had refused the request; but after they had retired to bed, she realized he was weeping. "I think we've just said no to the Lord," he explained. "We promised Him that this home would be dedicated to caring for children. My own dad was an alcoholic. What if somebody had said no to me?" The phone rang the other way the next morning with news for ECFA that a home had, indeed, been found for Jimmy.

Some of our commitments to the neglected children of the

world may be no more than supporting a child vicariously through one of the many Christian organizations which funds overseas orphanages—or we may find ourselves actually adopting some of these offspring from underprivileged or war-torn lands.

One couple we know had a special burden to share themselves with the oriental people. They promised each other they would adopt one child for every one of their three natural children.

Once the decision had been made, it was not so easy to carry out the task since there was such resistance from the agencies they contacted. With one of the adopted children, assistance from U.S. Senators was a necessary part of the red tape. Through the years the vow was fulfilled. But all three children, found at different places in different years, are the same age and in the same grade in school!

"You must be very certain this is something the Lord requires you to do, because of all the difficulties which may occur in bringing others into your immediate family," related this woman. *"And it must be a decision both you and your husband make.* One person shouldn't be imposing a pet desire on the other."

A firm verification from the Lord, and great patience were required in this case, since the first child suffered from diarrhea for a year and a half before the cause of the condition could be discovered and cured. These decisions must be based on "knowing strongly" that the Lord has asked you to do this hard thing, to hold this child screaming in nightmares for the third time this night, for the 12th consecutive night; to "know strongly" when that teenage girl given into your keeping doesn't return home one evening; to know when hostility occurs because of the huge reservoir of mistrust in one little life. We must know that Christ has asked us to walk this way, because often the road is rocky and steep and full of danger.

Then, when one bends his head and in childlike simplicity

148

asks Jesus to "come into my heart," when tension melts, when distrustful eyes are softened, when someone reports, "Boy! if they'd had work like this in that hospital, I would never have stayed sick!"—then each uncertain step was worth it all. Then, we would willingly face a dozen more sleepless nights. Then comes heart-shouting praise. Then rushes love; then the world shines.

The first time my eyes were opened to the challenge of using one's home for this special brand of hospitality was when my husband was the assistant pastor of a large church in the city. We came to know one outstanding family who ministered unusually with their home. With nine children of their own, and two foster children, they nevertheless ran what was practically a boarding house for missionaries' children—there were always three or four living with them whose parents were on the field. Add to this Grandpa, several international students, maybe a missionary family home on furlough, and you just might taste a sampling of what went on in this household.

The father was a doctor, well established and highly respected in his field, who was able to afford a large enough dwelling to house this menagerie of personalities. I laugh when I remember one of the teens saying, "You know, if it weren't for all of us kids, Dad would probably be pretty well off!" His wife—well, she knew the Lord had called her to be a mother, but her heart mothered worldwide.

Sunday afternoon dinners were kind of "bring whomever you want" affairs, and David and I were invited to sit down on frequent occasions at one of the tables to enjoy a life-style which up to this time had been foreign even to our imaginations. The house was well lived in—imagine organizing all the coats and boots and gloves and hats and mittens required by our midwestern winters—but the important things that needed doing were submitted to definite systems of organi-zations.

We will never live in that manner. We aren't called to it, but my vision of the ministry of hospitality was expanded tremendously through the influence of these people, and I am grateful to the Lord for allowing me to have been exposed to them.

Life Response

Do some consciousness-raising as to the plight of children in your community. Question a social worker. Investigate which charitable organizations place foster children. Inquire about statistics, and the availability of placement homes, and procedures in juvenile courts. Remember: just a little learning can be a dangerous thing.

14

The Hospice

MANY BESIDES CHILDREN NEED "HIDING PLACES" for short or longer periods of time. Circle Church people have made tentative experiments in opening their homes to adults whose lives need psychological restructuring, to unwed mothers needing a refuge, to lonely singles feeling the weight of social isolation.

We are learning that, while there are some who heal spontaneously in a hospitable shelter, there are others whose brokenness is so demanding it will take all we can give. It is important with these individuals to establish a living ratio of three healthy adults to one distressed personality. The task of rebuilding lives, giving support and discipline, acting in the sometimes preposterous role of substitute parent, is too demanding for one person or even one couple to supply.

I would never take an emotionally fragmented person into my home unless I was certain my marriage was on an absolutely solid basis with evidence of spiritual growth. Faced with a live-in counselee, David and I quickly discovered there were areas in our relationship we had tacitly agreed to overlook, slight personality flaws which were widening like a crack in the plaster. Patchwork was required, but we had been too busy looking in other directions to apply the proper attention. Everything suddenly surfaced when we added another personality to our living circumstances. Our comfortably passive coexistence became polarized by the presence of this difficult, psychologically damaged housemate. The living experiment was borne with difficulty as well as grace. We are personally grateful that light was thrown on the problems because we were forced to deal with them—as well as minister to a demanding broken personality to whom we had given shelter. But if our marriage had been less healthy, the "sandpaper effect" might have placed it under a great deal of undue strain.

Dealing with emotionally distressed personalities is a commitment which demands wisdom, discernment, humor, time, love, anger utilized at well-chosen moments, and honesty. It is obviously not an easy task. On the other hand, there are certain kinds of growth we experience in these live-in circumstances which cannot be known in any other. David and I have learned about the meaning of good parenting. We have lost our fear of disordered personalities. We have seen suffering on a moment-to-moment basis, and learned to apply our understanding in dealing with others who are in the same kinds of pain. We believe adamantly in the grace and miracle-work of God, because we have seen it overcome where we had prejudged someone to be "hopeless."

Each of us must examine these words from Isaiah and inquire if this is the kind of hospitality that the Lord is asking of us:

> "I want you to share your food with the hungry and bring right into your own homes those who are helpless, poor and destitute. Clothe those who are cold and don't hide from relatives who need your help. If you do these things, God will shed his own glorious light upon you. He will heal you; your godliness will lead you forward, and goodness will be a shield before you, and the glory of the Lord will protect you. Then, when you call, the Lord will answer. 'Yes, I am here,' he will quickly reply."
>
> *Isaiah 58:7-9, Living Bible*

David and I had been looking at the meaning of these verses for several weeks when the Lord brought that certain "child" into our lives. We were deeply convicted that opening our home was the thing He wanted us to do. From this "knowing" has come both the pain and the beauty of that experience.

When we are doing the hard works of redemption in this world we must be willing to walk behind that Gospel plow despite the disapproving nods around us. And if we are Christian we must cleanse our hearts from the creeping secular attitudes of chauvinism, provincialism and materialism which keep us from exercising a sacrificial, Christlike love. Francis Schaeffer, the founder of L'Abri fellowship in Switzerland, a community which has ministered Christ to the disenfranchised intellectual, talks about exercising this type of costly hospitality.

L'Abri is costly. If you think what God has done here is easy, you don't understand. It's a costly business to have a sense of community . . .

In about the first three years of L'Abri all our wedding presents were wiped out. Our sheets were torn. Holes were burned in our rugs. Indeed once a whole curtain almost burned up from somebody smoking in our living room. Blacks came to our table. Orientals came to our table. Everybody came to our place. It couldn't happen any other way. Drugs came to our place. People vomited in our rooms, in the rooms of Chalet Les Melezes which was our home, and now in the rest of the chalets of L'Abri.

How many times has this happened to you? You see, you don't need a big program. You don't have to convince your session or board. All you have to do is open your home and begin. And there is no place in God's world where there are no people who will come and share a home as long as it is a real home.

How many times have you risked an unantiseptic situation by having a girl who might easily have a sexual disease sleep between your sheets? We have girls come to our homes who have three or four abortions by the time they are 17. Is it possible they have venereal disease? Of course. But they sleep between our sheets. How many times have you let this happen in your home? Don't you see this is where we must begin? This is what the love of God means. This is the admonition to the elder—that he must be given to hospitality. Are you an elder? Are you given to hospitality? If not, keep quiet. There is no use talking. But you can begin . . .

If you have never done any of these things or things of this nature, if you have been married for years and years and had a home (or even a room) and none of this has ever occurred, if you have been quiet especially as our culture is crumbling about us, if this is so—do you really believe that people are going to hell? And if you really believe that, how can you stand and say, "I have never paid the price to open my living place and do the things that I can do"?

The compensations of this type of radical hospitality are often completely underestimated. For one friend unexpected resistance came from her Christian mother: "What will your neighbors think if you take that troubled personality to live in your home?" Quite contrary to those expressed fears, the neighbors soon recovered from their surprise, viewed closely some of the costly struggles of this dedicated family, and witnessed the marvelous end results. Their admiration was boundless. They had viewed in action a Christianity about which, before this demonstration, they had only heard words.

The question one might ask in considering the self-sacrifice required to minister this radical hospitality is, "Why is it necessary?" The answer is simply that there are some people who cannot be helped unless there are others who will open up their lives in this way.

In Jerusalem there is a large war memorial built to commemorate the hundreds of thousands of Jews who met their deaths in the holocaust of the insane Nazi inferno. Not a name is written on this building, but the street leading to this monument is called the Avenue of the Righteous. Here tree after tree after tree has been planted in living memory of those who aided the oppressed descendants of Abraham—courageous men and women who refused to capitulate to human law because they recognized the existence of a higher spiritual law.

Philosophers have often wondered how good people could stand by and allow such outrageous suffering—ignorance? hidden racism? helplessness? cowardice? Perhaps they were just out of practice. We in America have not yet been forced under such extreme circumstances to make these ultimate moral decisions. Perhaps, if that time comes, we will be so out of practice, holding so dearly to our earthly possessions—my home, my country, my race, my nationality—that we too will stand incapacitated in the face of great evil.

I wonder if there is an Avenue of the Righteous in Heaven where trees of life are planted to remember those here on earth who have provided hostels and hospices for the disembodied of our land? Is there a tree for those who chip away at the mountain of racism by sharing their lives with black brothers and sisters? Is there a tree for those who bear cups of sanity to the mentally ill? Is there a tree for those who care for little children? Is there a tree for those who open their doors to those refugees from another kind of war, that of light against darkness?

When we are given to hospitality we can become missionaries without leaving our homes, by inviting international students to live with us. We can become social workers without the frustration of bureaucracy. We can help to break racial barriers (if both sides chip and chip and chip away, one day that wall is going to fall) by marching in demonstration through our front doors. We can become way-stations for workers wearied by ministry.

My own spiritual life was radicalized by one missionary who

155

stayed with us for several days. This person's brand of faith was unlike any I had ever encountered. A witness to the reality of God in our lives was given that influences me to this day.

Another missionary couple and their two children lived with us for a month and demonstrated a style of marriage important for David and me to observe at that particular time. Due to their responsibilities on the field, they had developed a natural and delightful shared-role type of relationship. Child-rearing and homemaking were divided equally between husband and wife.

I recall thinking how well-adjusted their young children seemed to be when they had every reason to be upset or insecure. The family had been traveling from spot to spot for over a year, unable to root in any one place, meeting new people, saying good-bye to those they had come to love, moving on. Yet the children were well behaved, cooperative, and excellently disciplined, as well as obviously developing distinctive and delightful personalities. Able to observe them firsthand, I concluded that much of this well being was due to the even amounts of attention they received from each parent. A relaxed mother not overwrought from the exhaustion of too much childcare or the wearing day-in-and-day-outness of menial responsibilities had to contribute greatly to her children's own happiness.

David and I have also been the recipients of such healing hospitality. On our sometimes rather fixed income we have greatly appreciated the beautiful homes Christian brothers wealthier than ourselves have openly shared. We've dug clams for chowder off tiny Oak Island in Long Island Sound, watched the clouds break over the mountains from a retreat in Colorado, roamed Salem, Massachusetts, on Halloween with our children, floated on a yacht in the clear Caribbean with Jamaica bejeweled on the horizon, viewed the World Champion Sled-Dog Races in 15-degree-below-zero weather in Alaska, picked Florida grapefruit from our host's trees in the back yard—all because of other Christians' hospitality toward us. How often our spirits have been turned again toward ministry by the release of these experiences.

Once after a weekend escape to a friend's house overlooking Lake Michigan I sighed, "Oh, I wish we had a place like that."

"We do," David reminded me without glancing from his paperwork. "You have been told you can come whenever you like. And we don't have the worry of monthly payments or upkeep." Really, it has often been this way. People make me feel that I am welcome to share in as much of their lives as I am able to enjoy, and then take some away in my heart to store for memory replays.

You can be a part of the work of the Kingdom though you may not be on the front lines. Think of yourself as a behind-the-lines supply depot, a resting place away from the heat of the battle. Find ways to use the good things the Lord has given to you to ease the battle-scarred veteran or that fresh young recruit. You will give much to them, and they will give to you heroic stories of the conflict, marvelous undertakings of the Commander-in-Chief, intimate knowledge of the direction the battle is raging.

Hospitality is an open heart as well as an open home. All of us must develop this attitude whether we feel the Lord would have us invite people into our homes twice a year or two hundred times a year. I am not concerned so much about the quantity of hospitality, but I am concerned about the attitudes from which our practice springs. We must all have hospitable hearts and must ask the Lord if He wishes us to be a part of that minority whom He will require to open their hearts and homes radically.

Whenever we begin to exercise hospitality in this way, it is best not to operate out of ignorance. We need to inform ourselves as much as possible, locate other people who have walked this way before, and welcome assistance. For instance, the first time we invited a black family who attended the

157

church to our own apartment, we parked in the back, went up the back stairs and in the back door—a normal procedure because of the few parking spots. Our black friends, however, had had the experience of, "Go to that back door, boy," and they thought we were pulling the same racial stunt they had known all their lives. Pre-information would have been helpful in preventing this gaffe. Fortunately we were able to eventually rectify this error by welcoming these people many other times to our front door.

Internationals often complain about Americans and their one-time relationships, opening homes for Thanksgiving or Christmas celebration, then never establishing contact again. There is a great desire on the part of these so far from home to adopt a family with whom they can share, learn our customs, develop a facility in our language. Many organizations seek to aid internationals while they stay here in America, giving legal advice regarding visas, job permits, etc. And most large universities have a foreign student advisor who would be willing to provide contacts or answer questions. Foreign mission boards would also be another source of cultural information which could help us prevent many of the insensitivities which can destroy relationships before they start.

I wonder often about Jesus' illustration that we are the light of the world, and then I think about that light invisible to the human eye but amazingly transmitted onto film, that spiritual light surrounding those sheltered in the Calcutta Home for the Dying in India. I think about all those missionaries who have picked abandoned children from garbage piles or from jungle edges or from the clay steps of their front porches. I think about the hospitable Christians of history, of Catherine Zell of Strassbourg in the Middle Ages who opened that city to the refugees of the Peasants' War and single-handedly administrated relief to these several thousand. I think of the unadvertised hundreds of Corrie ten Booms, now trees of the righteous, who throughout centuries have sheltered the displaced, the life-hounded. I wonder what kind of illumination they have sent against the darkness.

What unseen incandescence rolls back the gloom when I open this my door and stand silhouetted against the warmth inside? Often I've wondered at the soft glow which fills the rooms only on hospitality nights. Is it candles? Is it my inward love toward these people making my eyes filmy? Or is it a Presence totally apart from myself, "the true light that enlightens every man"? What shadows are actually dispelled when we share Him with those in bondage, those with broken spirits, those strangers in prisons of their own making?

When I open my door do I send unseen rays to dispel the night? When I open my eyes and see the suffering, is my soul flooded with an unknown shimmering because I am seeing now with the eyes of Christ? When I open my heart, does it shine somewhere like the flame in a cavern, one living pinprick warding off the monstrous cavity of nothingness? Am I a light in the world, and is this house set on a hill for the city to see? I hope so. I fervently hope so.

Life Response

Take some tentative steps toward worldwide hospitality.

1. Contact a foreign student advisor to inquire as to whether there is a need for people to provide the atmosphere of a substitute family for internationals.

2. Give the church secretary your name to call the next time she needs someone to provide overnight housing for missionaries returning from the field.

15

Stewards of Time

BY NATURE I AM AN INSTINCT-IMPULSE PERSON, preferring to do things when I "feel" like it. For years I cleaned the house stimulated by the thought that company was coming, wrote because of a certain mood, and was easily able to lay aside planned operations when the zoo suddenly seemed more inviting or the Lake Michigan shore was beckoning.

David, on the other hand, is by nature an organized-compulsive. He feels most comfortable when the day is plotted to the minute, when every conceivable activity is on a list, when he is able to chart ahead and thereby determine how much time he will have in order to accomplish all his work.

These differences are most easily illustrated in the methods by which we both prefer to vacation. I would love to simply get in the car, follow the road, stop where I feel like stopping, meander here, explore there, and let the vacation happen to me. My husband, however, derives as much pleasure from the pre-plan as he does from the actual event. Road maps are spread on the table, atlases consulted, tourist guides and chamber of commerce information requested months ahead of time, itineraries planned, special sights to see chosen, tickets purchased, and friends we love who live on the way contacted in advance. David makes the vacation happen.

We have bumped more than frequently on this fundamental divergence in our characters. David's lists are endless, and for many years it was his habit upon rising first thing in the morning to organize his stacks of notes and papers for the day. I've teased him many a time about the esoteric shorthand he uses on these lists—"K K," I've wheedled. "I'll bet that means kiss Karen. You even have to program me into your systems!"

My jesting was not far from the truth. If I suddenly received the inspiration to take a walk, some inward journey demanding outward response, and if I decided it would be nice to be accompanied by a chatty or pensive husband to match my mood—David would have to consult his schedule to see if it fit in! Asking him to reserve next Thursday at 2:00 p.m. for a stroll simply didn't satisfy my need to follow impulses. By next Thursday, I wouldn't feel like taking a walk! After grumbling for many years about this work compulsion, one day I took a good look at us and had to admit that, David was accomplishing the work of ten men, reaching goals, affecting many lives, whereas I was gaining headway in virtually nothing.

It seemed as though I was always behind, always catching up on the housecleaning, the laundry, the decorating. I would stay up late to prepare for company the next day or get up in the wee hours to be ready to welcome people for dinner in the evening. I was always behind! My life was racing toward 30 and without a doubt I was trapped by trivia. Somehow I got only the unimportant things in my life done. I wanted to write; I wanted to learn; I wanted to make significant contributions as a Christian in our society, and here I was expecting (unexpectedly) our fourth child. I was even behind on that!

I realized the basic difference between David and myself was in our viewpoint of time. My husband had learned (albeit a little too well) how to be in control of time. On the other hand, time had always been in control of me. I thought back to the overdue term papers, the unwritten letters, the belated reports, and I suddenly became avowed—a deep, firm commitment that even if I died in the effort I would become organized, disciplined and motivated.

Looking long and hard at time—this one unalterable, precious gift which we cannot change, but only learn to use well, I asked, "Am I being a good steward of my time?" Once I began to perceive what time was, how it could be used or wasted, and what the Lord wanted me to do with it, my whole life started to change. Time was extremely important in determining the kind of ministry of hospitality I exercised.

Setting that summer aside so that I could learn how to manage my time, I first found it necessary to spend several weeks learning what I presently did with each moment of the day. A notebook provided me with that daily information, because into it I recorded each activity, logging the amount of time I devoted to each. I became aware of something I suppose I already knew subconsciously—I wasted hours of each day by not finishing tasks I had started or failing to begin the projects which most needed to be done. I was a dreamer, a passive uncontrolled thinker, an unsystemetized reader, a loafer.

From this point my goal became *to discipline myself to become disciplined.* With all honesty I must admit it was comparable to changing the course of tumbling water in midstream. As I began to progress, there were even a few sighs for the impulsive life.

After logging my time, I began to work the entire summer on developing schedules, systems, attacks and approaches to keeping an orderly house. The home was my primary area of responsibility, and it was the one I felt I had to conquer first before I could go on to anything else. A seminarian lived with us throughout those warm months and I blush even now to think what a continual gripe I was in that summer. In fact, I was a literal grump for the first six months of that pregnancy.

I ordered myself around, tackled the ramshackle closets and drawers, marched children in and out of how-to-clean sessions, drew up a daily schedule, and, with teeth gritted, forced us all to stick with it. I had to be mean and angry in order to motivate myself! By 9:00 a.m. rooms were to be straightened, everyone dressed, breakfast over, and the kitchen clean. From 9:00 to 10:00 the children owed Mommy one hour of work after which they disappeared to play. I continued to struggle over the baked-on mess in the oven, or the mountainous pile of ironing, or the upholstery project I had started months ago.

Through all this we carried on our usual open house—I remember because of the maternity hostess gown I wore. However, I began to practice some noticeable simplifications, abbreviations which were good lessons to apply toward the even busier days ahead.

Soon summer was over, the seminarian had departed, the older children were off to school, and just in time, as I was nearing the end of a rough pregnancy. For the last three months there was no hospitality. I had all I could do to scrape a meal together, and finally David took over even this detail.

Since Abraham put Sarah away privately when she was with child, I felt as though we in decency should do no less, and for those last few months I remained home from church, grateful for the few morning hours of silence. As I shuffled down the stairs, lumbered slowly from room to room, and gingerly pushed toys to where I could scoop them up with a broom, I began to see the benefits of those angry months. By hook and by crook I had become an orderly and disciplined housekeeper!

"Am I being a good steward of my time?" is a question which needs frequent evaluation. After I came home with a new baby, different schedules had to be maintained, and with each phase of my life new systems have to be developed. Good time management depends on the priorities we have chosen.

Dr. Ted Engstrom of the *Managing Your Time* seminars has reduced this process to a slogan—"goals, priorities and planning." My *goal* for that long summer was to become a disciplined housekeeper. This also became my *priority*, particularly in the face of my advancing pregnancy, despite the rooming-in student, the work of hospitality, the expeditionary jaunts with the children. The *planning* evolved through first of all logging how I employed what time I had, then setting up schedules and assigning tasks to other members of the family.

After all this had been accomplished, the Lord did a lovely thing for me in that eighth-floor hospital room in the maternity ward. He gave me a retreat. I watched the winter clouds scudding grayly above the foaming winter waters of Lake Michigan, studied the concrete and asbestos towers of the city, and wondered why no one came to fill the other bed in this large room with a lovely view. There in that quiet I began to devour my new Living Bible. Despite tranquilizers, I was unable to sleep and would turn to the bedside table and read with delight. The Lord planted then in my heart a seed which one day grew into a voracious hunger for Himself.

Looking back through the years to that summer, I can see many a time when I employed this method of goal setting, establishing priorities, and then planning how to reach them. With each step of progress He increased my usefulness until finally the day came when I realized our time is really His time. Now each day begins with an inquiry of the Lord, "These are my human plans. Is this what You want me to do?"

The *goal* for this time in my life is to finish several writing projects. The exercise of the gift of writing has taken precedence over those other abilities of ministry which have been given to me. My list of *priorities* in order are: 1. My relationship to the Lord. 2. My relationship to my husband. 3. My role of mothering the children. 4. Finishing the writing projects. 5. Relating to the needs of my parents. 6. Keeping the house in order. 7. The work of the church.

Planning to reach this goal includes setting aside three or four large time blocks each week to write, calling on help for baby-sitting, finding ways to survive on the simplest, quickest meals possible, and attending the barest minimum of outside functions. I am fast becoming a recluse, and I have haunting feelings that when I emerge no one will be there who remembers me! Hospitality for the first time in our married lives is down to a minimum. I find I cannot write about hospitality and be hospitable at the same time.

Choosing between our goal and the planning which enables us to reach the goal can be one of our most frustrating tasks. As Christians this means we must not only know who we are, but also what God is expecting us to be and do. Getting to know oneself is a lifelong process, and knowing God is a matter that takes eternity; yet it is only as we get to know ourselves as well as the God who transcends us that we can discover our unique reasons for being, or our goals.

The pursuit of person must begin. We must all ask, "What is it I want to do or be?" For many of us that question can also be worded, "What is it I am *meant* to do or to be?" The Lord may require that I make the largest thrust of my time the molding of little lives and hearts. To others He gives additional trusts, and we find we are required to juggle many roles and to juggle them well.

I know that I am an instinct-impulse person with an endurance run of about two weeks. I can push myself to the limit for only about that long, after which I need a time of solitude, with several days to do the things I want to do, not the things I have to do. When our first child was born, I learned early that I did not want to *change* his basic nature. Rather I wanted to help him *channel* his basic personality and God-given gifts. This is true for myself also. I may establish strict disciplines for my life, but within those guidelines there must be ebb and flow, freedom from long-range, minute-to-minute responsibilities, provision for enough aesthetic input. I do not wish to change what I am, only to channel it better so that I can function fully.

Some sacrifices must be made. I no longer have time for leisurely shopping expeditions, long afternoons in art museums, or frequent luncheons with friends. When the portable television was dropped by one of the children it found its way to the junk pile shop because it was a time gobbler.

Establishing priorities is essentially a matter of making choices. In six months the choices will be different. There will be time for the personal counseling I enjoy, for speaking engagements, for long walks going nowhere, for the intellectual feeding from library shelves, for taking a high school growth group, and for my greatest of all loves, the open door with people in every room, with food well-prepared, candles glowing, and laughter and love.

The amount of time available to us determines the quantity and personality of our hospitality. Up until recently David and I have carried on an extensive ministry of availability almost every day of the week. When we were led to devote so much time to people who lived with us, the ministry of an open house began to diminish. Now both David and I have priority activities which require long hours of seclusion. We have had to refrain temporarily from the style of former days, participating sometimes in nothing more than hospitable attitudes. I can now sympathize with those people who have such consuming work that they have to state, "I don't have the time or the energy to be hospitable."

On the other hand, there are people who can devote large amounts of time and energy to hospitality. The temptation which always accompanies this situation is to do more than is required. It is easy to spend days in elaborate preparations which have nothing to do with ministry but a great deal to do with demonstrating one's own abilities. One must look carefully at those hidden motives and ask, "Am I really seeking to serve, or am I trying to impress?"

A good thermometer as to whether pride was rising in me was to ask two questions: Am I nervous? Am I fussing? These were pretty good indicators of the true nature of my intentions. If I was nervous, getting jumpy before that sit-down dinner for eight, I could assume something had gone awry within. Was I afraid the new recipe would flop, or that someone might wander into an unclean room—and people would think less of me?

For me nervousness stemmed from nothing more than pride.

What did it matter if the centerpiece was less than spectacular, if the rolls were slightly more than brown on the bottom, if the door to the little boys' room was closed because to enter was to take one's life in one's hands?

If I found myself fussing too much about spots on the glasses, getting upset because I had to clean the bathroom sink *again*, going wild because someone had walked on the freshly vacuumed shag—what did it mean? Who was coming that I was trying to impress with all these efforts? Didn't my over-concern indicate that I was depending on my human efforts to make the evening a success? Hadn't I forgotten that undefinable spiritual quality which found its source in the Holy Spirit? Again the answer was pride, pride rearing its subtle and manipulative head, forcing me to think self.

To me maturing has been a lengthy process of letting go— letting go of props that bolster one's ego, letting go of ploys and gambits that vault us in the eyes of other people, letting go of many of the material means that become so important in our eyes. How lovely to be able finally to laugh at our disasters!

I remember one sultry summer evening in our third-floor apartment. It was the third week of a Chicago heatwave. Even the bare wood floor had absorbed the warmth. The curtains were muggy. The breeze off the lake barely stirred the sycamore leaves in the courtyard. Instead of using the oven, I chose to serve a cold salad dinner and ran to the nearby grocer to purchase an assortment of ice cream bars for dessert.

At the end of the main course, I slipped into the kitchen and pulled the sack of popsicles and ice cream bars from the freezer. To my dismay I discovered it was so warm they hadn't refrozen. Peeling the soggy wrappers from each one I had no choice but to put away my pride, scoop the sloppy messes into individual bowls, accent them with their wooden sticks as a clue as to what they had once been, and serve them to the puzzled guests. Matters were complicated because a melted ice cream bar is considerably smaller than a frozen one and my cereal bowls were rather large. I could do nothing but laugh and pass the spoons. I'm still laughing now.

Turkeys have always been my Waterloo. On our first Thanksgiving we invited both sets of grandparents to celebrate the traditional meal in our honeymoon apartment. The moment they walked up the stairs it was as though someone had released a smoke bomb in the kitchen. Our flat was inundated. Smoky fumes seeped from one room to another. Choking, but mustering as much aplomb as possible, I ushered each set of grandparents into our bedroom, seated them on the bed to get acquainted, and closed the door to protect them from the acrid atmosphere. Then, gasping and heaving for air, David and I rushed about throwing open windows, flapping the billows of smoke out with towels, leaning our heads out windows for a breath of fresh air, then plunging back to battle. This process was complicated by the fact that David and I were laughing uncontrollably.

Finally the air cleared. The turkey was unimpaired. It had simply been too large for its pan and the juices had leaked into the broiler pan, which smoked happily ever afterward whenever heated and had to finally be discarded. If I remember correctly it was a decent enough first Thanksgiving meal. But my grandfather put the *coup de grace* on it ten years later when he reminded me of the event. "Do you know, Karen Sue," he revealed most confidentially, "I never told anyone about it." Appreciating his honorable intent, it was now my turn to keep a confidence. He never knew that his valor was unnecessary since I had revealed this disgraceful incident to at least a few thousand people myself.

There is nothing wrong with serving things elegantly. I recall one friend rebuking me when I had gone overboard on a simplicity kick by saying, "I love it when people go to extra efforts. It makes me feel as though they have a special reason to do so much for me."

I needed to hear those words, and ever since have taken that attitude when I am on the receiving end of hospitality. I have learned to enjoy the work of another's hands. However, I have personally found great freedom in guarding my own motives, being sure that extra frills stem from a desire to give, to minister, rather than from a desire to impress.

Am I being a good steward of my time? is a question which starts many a journey. Witness my own marriage. I am well on my way to becoming a compulsive worker just as my husband is finally traveling in the opposite direction toward the light-hearted, impulsive decade of 40! Yet, with laughter aside, it is an inquiry of magnitude. One that has not only helped to form the dimensions of my gift of hospitality, but has defined the parameters of my personality as well. I am becoming a good manager of my time, and through that, of my life.

Life Response

1. An excellent book on time management for Christian women has been written by Pat King. It is titled, *How Do You Find the Time,* and can be ordered from:

   Aglow Publications
   7715 236th SW
   Edmonds, WA 98020

2. If you have never charted your time or activities, do so now. Buy a notebook and log the way your precious days pass. Continue this for several weeks in order to gain a fair understanding.

3. Also take a few moments to list your personal goals. What is it you want to do with your life? What things are important?

16

Shortcuts

Most of us don't have all the time we want to carry on ministries of hospitality. We seek to discover shortcuts so that we can open our homes with a minimum of effort. Through the years certain basic principles have been helpful in allowing me to combine an open home with the other complicated demands on my time.

The first one is: *Never clean before company*. Once I had established a system of housekeeping, it was not necessary to make the house spotless before people arrived. I didn't clean for people, I cleaned on schedule. This has freed enormous quantities of time. For many years all I did was get ready for groups and pick up after them. Finally I have learned that things don't need to be spotlessly clean, only in order. When things are in order, people are not going to notice if the rug was not vacuumed that morning. And even if they do, they will probably feel more at home. I have invariably made close friends when they saw dishes stacked in the kitchen, or dust on the piano, or fingerprints on the front door!

I follow this rule so adamantly that I save my cleaning routine for after company is gone—the housekeeping is scheduled for Saturday morning after the late Friday night potluck dinner. Obviously I make clean sheets available for overnight guests—but I am not above stripping the mattress and asking those same people to put the fresh linen on it for me. The guest bathroom is refreshed after the sand-and-peanut-butter crowd, but I am not a fanatic, since spotlessness is impossible as long as there is grit and goo to wash off little hands.

The second rule builds on the first: *Don't be afraid to do things with flair*. An old patchwork quilt for a table cloth, huge baskets of dried fall weeds, a stylish hostess gown (no matter if it's a hand-me-down as long as it *looks* good)—only one or two old dependables with class can cover a multitude of cleaning errors. Flair is a creative expression God has imprinted on our souls. Yet we Christians are wary of those dramatic touches of finesse. God is not afraid to display His creativity. If we did one room in our home copying the glorious colors in just one of His sunsets, people would think we were outrageous. Yet He has donned His world with style and class and exquisite taste and breathtaking color combinations and scintillating humor—have you ever looked at the rear end of a baboon! And He allows this repetition of glory and delightful surprise in His human creature, as long as we don't slip into the error of thinking it is all of ourselves.

Old wooden bowls and the variegated patterns of baskets intrigue me. I use them as serving pieces. I love to provide fresh fruits in place of heavy, sweet desserts. Their appetizing colors are delightful, the yellows and oranges and purples juxtaposed against the grains of an antique hand-turned basin satisfy some unknown need in me. For *flair* I add crumpled, wizened figs on a string which I buy from a Greek grocer.

Recently several of us were recalling special touches of class our mothers practiced. My mother had a gift for last-minute inspiration. She worked, managed a big house, raised three kids, and loyally supported her high-pressure husband, who invariably involved us all in his choirs, recitals, retirement schemes, and other plans. Consequently, her entertaining was off the cuff, spur of the moment. I lovingly recall the clean-the-refrigerator affairs on Sunday evening after church—the food was served hodge-podge on the kitchen table, but it had a personality all its own—the oyster stew suppers eaten off trays before the log-laden fire, the summer watermelon wedges glowing pink, green, and pearl piled in a basket.

David remembers his mother always serving beautifully. Mom is a woman with incredible energy who has established what for most would be impossible standards. She serves even casual snacks with placemats. Her home is a visual delight. I once asked my husband if he remembered her in anything but high heels, and he laughed with the memory of her scrubbing a floor in heels and earrings looking like a queen. This is flair that is organized, controlled and splendid. It is classic Oriental antiques and polished surfaces and mellow lighting. It is "nothing is worth doing without doing well." It is a treat.

Someone else commented on how his mother had served playmates peanut butter and jelly sandwiches—cut in wedges, resting on a white doily which was perched on a silver plate. That is definitely *flair.* We each will develop our own style, but let us do it with delight, remembering Who is the source of these waiting-to-be-discovered homemaking triumphs.

Rule number three: *Do as much ahead of time as possible.* Once my approach to homemaking became more orderly, when I sat down and planned a week rather than allowing each day to just happen, I could foresee setting aside special time in preparation for a special event. Frozen salads could be mixed on Tuesday, the chicken divan prepared Thursday evening and refrigerated, the dessert baked some morning after breakfast, when all the accumulated dishes could be washed at the same time. Friday's dinner became a breeze. Nothing is more satisfactory than to be able to take a nap on the afternoon of an event, or to spend the morning at the library with the children.

In fact, because my schedule is now necessarily tight, doing ahead has become a game. I collect those recipes which do not require last-minute preparation—souffles are *out*! I treasure foods which look great, taste terrific, but which require a minimum of kitchen time. The trusted old standbys are utilized frequently. I test myself against the ease of a hospitality occasion. Hard work indicates that I am slipping back into old habits, running behind, not managing my time well, not planning or preparing ahead, doing too much, not being dependent on the Lord's strength, but on my own. An aching back is a sure sign that I need to reevaluate.

Rule number four: *Clean as you go.* This is the cardinal principle to orderly management. Leave a room as ordered as you found it. Straighten up before you retire for bed at night. Clean pots and pans and utensils directly after use. I have developed a system whereby I wash the dishes after each course of a large party. The kitchen is already straightened from last-minute preparations. The punch cups are washed after the children have collected them and people are sitting in the living room talking; the salad and dinner plates are cleared by the children while I scrape and wash and stack. All that remains is dessert silverware and plates, goblets, coffee and tea cups, serving dishes. A major portion of the cleanup is accomplished before the last course, at which time I relax, enjoy the conversation, and think about how little there is left to do.

Rule number five: *Use all the help that comes your way.* Gone forever are the days when I'd rather do it myself. I have learned about the inestimable value of helping hands. If someone asks, "Is there anything I can do for you?" I will probably respond, "Yes!" In fact, there is something so satisfactory about sharing work with a friend, coordinating an evening for a large group in conjunction with someone else's gifts and ideas that I will probably never again attempt to solo navigate through another huge affair!

Many a pleasurable evening has been co-hostessed with other women in the church. These have become opportunities for knowing one another as well as ministering. A friend and I once recognized that many new couples needed to become acquainted with each other. We jointly planned a crepe dinner. We each flipped one hundred of these thin French pancakes, served punch for the appetizer, a sauce of mushrooms, ham and sour cream for the main dish, and several choices—raspberry and peach melba, butterscotch and almonds, something chocolate—for dessert. She provided chafing dishes and extra utensils, a large coffee server and placemats. My contribution was the home and the beverages. We set up tables in every room downstairs, with punch bowls in several places, and enjoyed the evening getting acquainted ourselves.

I am no longer afraid to ask someone to toss the green salad I didn't have time to put together, or to fry bacon for those hurried after-church brunches. My family has learned to lend invaluable assistance. They rally in that last hour before guests arrive—David takes care of dinner music and "licks and promises," the getting-children-presentable detail; Randall is in charge of ice and water; Melissa arranges appetizers and serves them; all are expected to be on standby in case of emergencies.

For breakfasts my husband is generally the chef-in-command, seeing as he has an eager hand with an egg and experience working as a short-order cook which includes skill in flipping pancakes, turning browned sausages, and rounding off ground meat patties just so.

When we regularly entertain for sit-down dinners, we often invite people to bring one course for the meal. One family is in charge of appetizers, another the salad, another the dessert. This leaves me responsible for the main dish, accompanying vegetables, and bread. Sometimes I ask for specific donations such as a fresh green salad, but more likely I just allow people to bring whatever the spirit moves them to conjure up.

A friend recently reminded me of an evening about which I had forgotten, the "bring-a-pie" night. About 40 were invited, half of whom brought marvelous home-baked delicacies. There was next to no work for me. I simply extended invitations, plugged in the coffee pot, mixed a cold fruit drink, and offered a welcome heart. I didn't even make a pie! There was no need with the buffet table groaning from a delectable array of 20 choices.

Rule number six: *Keep files.* Four file drawers filled with folders stuffed with clippings is often the secret of my avowed creativity. There is an envelope for "Organizational Ideas," for "Economy—Food," for "Breakfasts" and "Main Dishes" and "Appetizers." One swift glance can provide me with enough stimulation for a month of creative and systematized hospitality. These files are the only way I can justify the expense of women's magazines.

I am learning that there is always time for the things the Lord wants us to do. The writings of Charles Williams opened my mind more than anything else to the fact that our God does not exist in a world of time the way we humans do. This English writer had the amazing ability of realistically combining the spiritual world with the material world. Each of his seven novels has the flavor of that Old Testament incident at Dothan where the prophet Elisha prayed that the eyes of his servants might be opened to see the fiery chariots and forces of the Lord. In *All Hallows' Eve* the city of death is superimposed upon the city of life, or, according to Williams, they "coinhere." The reader's mind is continually stretched to look at time in ingenious and in more-than-human ways.

I like to think of time as a capsule spinning out in space. In this protective enclosure man exists. Outside is the vast universe into which he makes tentative explorations, discovering that there the aging process is slowed. Time is a human dimension, not a godly one. God cannot be contained by time.

Scripture proclaims in Isaiah that He is "the high and lofty one who inhabits eternity." God is outside the capsule, beyond our limited concept of time. One thousand years are as but a day in His sight. Our minds are boggled at the mathematics required to communicate this incomprehensible dimension. Yet that very universe is somehow contained for, by, and within Him.

Ecclesiastes tells us, "He has planted eternity in our hearts." What the ramifications of this may be are hard to tell. Perhaps there is an inner yearning to be beyond time, a continual struggle for immortality, for example, in the dictator, perverted as he seeks to strike lasting notches in finite time. I see some of this struggle in myself, yet there is more. Daily I experience, when I am doing the work He has set me to do, His manipulation of this human element to increase my usefulness for Himself.

He orders our days, to be sure. When each morning we make the daily oblation, that sacrificial prayer offering ourselves as servants for His sake, most of us can testify to His going ahead, charting, making paths clear, bringing the right people to the right place at the right time. Yet there is even more. I think He gives us tastes of eternity, moments stretched allowing us to do more than we ever expected, 20 minutes of sharing in which we plumb the depths of another soul at a level normally requiring years. How often after rising early, spending time in His Presence, and committing the activities of His day to planning, have I looked in amazement at the clock which should by rights read 11:30 according to all that has been accomplished, only to discover it is just 9:00. In some strange way, when we are about His business, He makes the eternity, about which we know so very little, work in our favor.

Each of us must learn to determine what is important in our lives. We must come to an agreement with the time which we have been allotted. If the Lord is asking us to carry on extensive ministries of hospitality, we will then be able to know the human limitations within which we work. We will learn to adjust our attitudes and discover shortcuts. We may also experience the supernatural. We may know when He is about the flowering of that planted eternity within our hearts.

Life Response

Develop some shortcuts of your own.

1. If you don't have a file system already, buy some folders and start clipping time-saving ideas. Be forewarned that discipline will be required—discipline to collect these useful hints as well as to employ them!

2. Invite a small group of people who lead similar life-styles to brainstorm on some shortcuts which will aid effective ministry. Use each other as resource material. It's amazing how many ideas can pop out of the head of five account executives (or homemakers, or farmers, etc.)!

17

Creativity and Simplicity

CREATIVITY HAS BEEN DEFINED as adventurous thinking. It is the ability to get away from the main track, break out of the mold, or diverge from the rest of society. In the previous chapters we have already viewed hospitality in a creative way. We have thought adventurously, seeing Christian hospitality as the opposite of "entertaining"—those prideful attempts to impress others. In this creative approach we have looked at hospitality as a gift of the Holy of Christ. Now let us continue to think adventurously and discover the specifics of hospitality.

Rollo May, the noted psychologist, writes in *The Courage to Create* that creativity requires limits. He reasons that the creative act "arises out of the struggle of human beings with and against that which limits them." I can easily identify my own limits to hospitality—finances, energy, time. These are legitimate strictures, thrust upon me by my circumstances. As a Christian I also have Scriptural limitations—Christ's injunctions about putting the Kingdom of God before our desire for material possessions, denying oneself, going the extra mile, and other mandates. What creative responses can come "out of the struggle with and against that which limits me"?

Many of you will not have the limitations which are mine—my grandmother at 88 has more energy than I have, others are blessed with unlimited financial resources, and time hangs heavy on many a hand—so I will share these creative struggles as examples, hoping they will stimulate ideas in areas of limitation other than my own.

For most of our life we have been in the ministry. Consequently, we have well-defined economic limits. By all rights, radical hospitality should have been an impossible burden. We have generally been given some expense remuneration, but our ministry far and away exceeds that allotment. To say the least, I have learned to be frugal. When we were living in the city, one of the daily papers published a scale of income rated per number of children and showing financial aid given to dependent mothers. I discovered that for a family of our size I was feeding us for less than what a mother on welfare was receiving for food.

I realized, of course, that I had paddings that many on welfare did not have: summer vegetables from my father's garden which we eventually learned to can for the winter, shared food from someone else's bounty, even the academic know-how to live economically. But even with this help, our continual open house should have been a strain. Yet we were managing well due to some creative approaches that we were employing. What were they?

More than at any other time, I learned how the Lord infuses His grace into our physical limitations, particularly when we are seeking to serve Him. How often, with a minimal supply and increasing demand, I can testify to His creating enough for all from fishes and loaves. Inspiration would come in that moment when I stared at the bare cupboard—"simply nothing to fix"—and suddenly! If I combined such-and-such with this-and-this I would have an original and tasty company dinner. A dozen eggs meant we could invite people for brunch. Someone would invariably inquire, "Can I bring anything?" and we would assign sausage or bacon. Bread was sliced for toast with home-preserved elderberry jelly. A fruit bowl and coffee would complete the meal. The remains of half a square of cream cheese cubed into the scrambled eggs, figs in the fruit, blue and white ironstone china, and old white restaurant mugs provided flair.

How often after inviting people home I had no idea what we could serve and would simply depend upon the Lord to provide. Someone would slip five dollars into David's coat pocket, or there would be just enough money to buy one certain ingredient which, when purchased, would round out an entire menu. For many years we received weekly two brown paper bags of day-old bakery goods, cakes for desserts, and sweet rolls for continental breakfasts. We never bought a loaf of bread in that entire time. My mother would run into a meat sale and share a pot roast with us which we would serve for a dinner of eight.

Trust is a lesson in adventurous thinking. Inviting people when you know you have nothing to serve, but depending on God to *always* supply, is adventurous living.

Every once in a while I became the recipient of large restaurant-size cans of food. A huge container of chicken salad became the staple for the makings for submarine sandwiches garnished with pineapple and mandarin oranges. These were served on two consecutive afternoons when I invited the women of the block to luncheons to celebrate with me the coming of spring. Everything the Lord gives to us can be given back to Him. Then He in turn blesses and breaks and creates from it a bounteous provision.

I am not above saying to people we love, "Let's have dinner together after church. I've got such-and-such in my refrigerator. What have you got in yours?" We have often enjoyed some odd but nevertheless nourishing meals together. And the spur-of-the-moment fellowship has been superb.

The rooms of our home are narrow and small. I was once the guest in a marvelous mansion nestled in the mountains where a gallery stretched the length of the front of the house, and where the light and shadow of the forest played continually in the rooms. The kitchen was almost as large as my downstairs,

181

and the living room was exquisite with its muted tones of soft pink and grays and beiges. My hostess, a lovely Christian woman, was sharing her plans for some social affair. Over a hundred guests were invited, and they would fit most comfortably into those elegant and spacious rooms. In kindness she turned to me and remarked, "But it really doesn't matter how much room you have, does it?"

I thought of my 13' x 13' living room, of the close quarters we experienced when we had a group of 30, of people sitting on floors and crowded into corners, of all six of us sleeping in the three upstairs bedrooms when we had two live-ins, and I laughed, good wholesome humor welling up in my heart, "Oh, yes it does!"

But my hostess was right. It really doesn't matter what size your rooms are. Somehow Christ expands the walls or compresses the people. We always seem to fit. It is the offering of what we have that counts, the depending upon Him to create more from what we give.

Some of my economic limits are self-imposed. When I look at many of the people in the city, or at those who suffer in this impoverished world, I often feel inordinately well off. My home with the tiny living room and its cramped city lot bordered by the back alley seems palatial when compared to the hovels of many in the world. In honor of these we have deliberately imposed limits on ourselves. Our meat meals, particularly beef, are limited. My children are being introduced to that protein staple of thousands, black beans, rice, and corn tortillas. Our garden with its rows and rows of vegetables is to me an important philosophical statement.

For some it may be a creative response to serve creamed chicken with dumplings rather than the easier broiled sirloins. If my Christian brother whom I invite, with a family of ten children and a low income, is out-classed by what I offer, made to feel as though he can never return the favor, then limitations need to be self-imposed. Of course, I need not be ridiculous and provide a meal ludicrously below my station, but I must be wise.

Simplicity is another self-imposed limitation for the Christian. Again I am referring primarily to an attitude. Once God's Kingdom has become our priority, we will not always need to be asking, "What shall we eat, or drink, or put on?" He will provide. Our hospitality can't help but be influenced. Putting Christ's Kingdom first will affect whom we invite, how we minister to them, and what we do with the material gifts added unto us after we establish this priority.

Simplicity finds its roots in this Kingdom mindset. We will deny ourselves participation in some forms of living for the sake of doing His work first in the world and of identifying with our Christian brothers. The ramifications of this priority will be different for each of us. For me it will mean one thing—serving economic stews and homemade soups and inviting guests to bring a variety of homebaked breads. For you it might mean another—spending the money to have an evening catered.

Putting His Kingdom before the other demands on our time and energy will also deliver us from living by comparison. In a world full of people attempting to keep up with the Joneses, this is another mark of adventurous thinking. If a Christian brother has more than I do materially, the Lord has given that to him, and I will not wish for what he has. I can give to those who have been kind to me out of what I have. I don't have to do the same thing for them that they did for me when I was last in *their* home.

If we find ourselves comparing, something is wrong. We are in danger of covetousness. Our attitude is not "Kingdom first." If it was we would be freed from this interior wanting. Simplicity is the greatest freedom.

Several years ago I realized there was a hungering thing in my heart, a too-much-caring after the goodly products of this world. I looked at our home, the unfinished rooms, the uncarpeted floors, the rickety, child-scarred furnishings, and realized that, with life being as it was, I was going to have to make a choice. The economics of our life demanded that all decorating projects be hand-turned or homemade, taking hours, even months of work. Either I was going to have to devote my time to becoming the spiritual woman I knew God was calling me to be, or I was going to have to spend years getting our home in a shape that would satisfy my taste in design, color and form. It was one or the other.

One afternoon I sat on the living room floor and flipped my Bible to that passage from Matthew about "worry not." I realized I had been worrying, fussing about bare walls and the lack of furniture, spending hours imagining cleverly finished rooms. The words from Scripture burned in my heart and I finally chose. "Kingdom first, Lord," I prayed. "I will put everything aside and become what You want me to be."

From that day I began to spend regular hours in studying the Word and in prayer. In order to prove the depth of my intent, I made several vows before the Lord. One was not to read anything but Scripture until I felt I had a working knowledge of that Book. This continued for a year. The other was to conduct a three-month shopping fast. I refused to enter any store but a grocery store, and I looked to the Lord to provide any needs beyond food.

The Lord always honors us when we take steps of faith before Him. The Word became alive and took form within my flesh. At the end of the three-month shoppingless period, our downstairs living and dining areas had been carpeted by the good graces of a parent, lovely old antiques had been discarded in my direction friends had dropped in to give us a hand emptying the paint buckets, their contents thickening in the basement—all at the stimulation of the Spirit, not because of our requests! Moreover, the Lord released me from that hungering thing. After a while it became easier to put the Kingdom first.

The hospitality we carried on during this time was simple, also. People brought parts of meals. I began to lean more to inexpensive breakfasts and later-evening cheese and fruit affairs.

I find that as I think creatively and become more yielded to the Spirit, I become sensitized to the world about me. Being freed from self guarantees participation in the lives of others.

We must learn to use our real limitations—those costly physical, emotional and financial drains—creatively. Kurt Hahn, father of Outward Bound, whose schools use wilderness training to engender self-initiative, developed a philosophy early in life when he spent a year in a darkened room after suffering from a severe form of sunstroke—"Your disability is your opportunity." We as Christians must use our disabilities as our opportunities. How can we meet the overwhelming needs of the world when there is so much pain and so few of us? How can we use our limited potentials to their utmost?

One creative answer is by combining them. An answer to ministering hospitality which has existed throughout the centuries has been the commune. Many Christians today are living together, sharing homes and incomes in order to free themselves to make significant contributions in society as well as in the church.

Forms of communal living can be established in a variety of ways. David and I have tasted community when we have had live-in guests. Individual families living in separate dwellings can make certain obligations to each other. They can promise to support and encourage and assist one another financially, by joining together for regular prayer and Bible study; they can establish food co-ops, share household equipment such as ladders and lawn mowers. The possibilities for this modified form of shared life are endless. If we learn to trade child-care responsibilities, aid one another in menial tasks, take turns preparing those thousands of yearly meals, can't our lives then be freed for more ministry, more growth, more becoming?

Not all creative applications of hospitality need to be revolutionary. In our dour and work-laden lives, an adventurous approach may be simply to plan an evening of delight and celebration.

One woman of the church reported to me that she and her husband were picking up my dropped ends of hospitality and were having informal get-togethers. I was relieved to hear this and surprised when she mentioned the names of several people I hadn't as yet met. "We had a progressive dinner last night," she reported. "And we're really pleased with the way everyone became so well acquainted."

"A progressive dinner? Who else's home did you use?" I wanted to know.

"Oh, no one's," she replied. "We progressed to the bedroom for the appetizer, to the dining room for the main course, and to the living room for dessert. This circulation mixed everyone together." This was to me another example of creative hospitality mixed liberally with delight.

We need to remember the whole first phrase from the Westminster *Shorter Catechism,* "The chief end of man is to glorify God *and enjoy him forever.*" Once we have established the right attitudes, we may minister with and be ministered to simply through laughter, joy and celebration.

How many limitations Christ experienced, and what an example of simplicity He set—"foxes have holes but the Son of man has nowhere to lay his head"! Yet what creative solutions He found to extend hospitality to a world which sought Him out. Bread for thousands from a few loaves, wine from water—all disabilities turned into opportunities. To all who came He gave Himself, rest for the weary, food for the hungry, water for the thirsty. Can we too learn to think as adventurously? Can we discover that hospitality is not what we have, but what we are? Can we give out of our limited resources only to find creativity rising out of that struggle "with and against that which limits us"?

Life Response

You may be convinced that you are not creative. Or perhaps you wish you could develop more in this area. Read the following list of blocks to creativity, then check the areas in which you think you are weak.

_____ *Fear of failure*—drawing back; not taking risks; settling for less in order to avoid the possible pain or shame of failing.

_____ *Reluctance to play*—overly serious approach to problem-solving. Fear of seeming foolish or silly by experimenting with the unusual.

_____ *Resource myopia*—failure to see one's own strengths; lack of appreciation for resources in one's environment.

_____ *Over-certainty*—rigidity of problem-solving responses; stereotyped reactions.

_____ *Frustration avoidance*—giving up too soon when faced with obstacles; avoiding discomfort associated with change.

_____ *Custom-bound*—overemphasis on tradition, too much reverence for the past; tendency to conform when not necessary.

_____ *Impoverished fantasy life*—overvaluing the so-called objective, real world; lack of imagination in the sense of being able to pretend or ask, "What if?"

_____ *Need for order*—Inability to tolerate disorder, confusion or ambiguity; dislike of complexity.

_____ *Reluctance to let go*—trying too hard to finalize solutions to problems; inability to let things incubate or happen naturally; lack of trust in human or supernatural capacities.

—— *Fear of paradox*—not making sufficient use of contrasting ways to reach the meaning of things; tendency to polarize to opposites, rather than knowing how to integrate the best of both sides; lacking perception of wholeness.

Take your checked areas before the Lord and ask Him to help you change so that you might think more adventurously.

18

At Ease

AUTHOR JEANNE HILL WRITES in a recent *Reader's Digest* that, while her mother was the one long on etiquette, insisting on flowers in the house as well as a white starched tablecloth and napkins for each evening meal, it was really her father who taught her the most significant lessons regarding manners. A 16-year-old Ozark lad had been hired to help dig out the storm cellar, and as the afternoon stretched into evening, he was invited to sit down at the family dinner.

A short passage was read from Scripture, prayer was offered, and everyone took up their forks. Everyone except this gangly teen—he picked up his knife. Noticing the custom of this house, he transferred eating utensils to copy the manner of the family, and soon beans and gravy tumbled awkwardly down his front.

An embarrassed silence began to grip the room, and just when it seemed as though nothing could redeem the situation, the author remembers her father laying aside his own fork, picking up his knife, and casually ladling both beans and gravy into his mouth. The evening was saved, and the hill-born lad happily resumed his familiar eating habit.

After the guest was gone, the father received much acclaim from other family members, but he turned the comments aside stating, "Good manners are nothing more than making the other person feel at ease."

As far as I am concerned, *etiquette is nothing more than making the other person feel at ease.* In developing social graces we must cultivate that instinct for knowing where the other person is, what he is feeling, how we can make him feel at home. We learn to notice who has not been participating in the conversation, and we find a question that will draw him in. We learn to hear those verbal clues to unhappiness, or we identify the body movement that signals someone is feeling uncertain or uncomfortable in our group.

For the Christian, good manners means having a Christlike mind which looks out for the interest and comfort of others before its own.

When we invite people into our homes, we must put away our pride, no longer seeking to impress but to serve. Whom do we invite? We look for those who are lonely, the young woman recently hospitalized whose family is half a world away. Would she like to recover from surgery in a home rather than a rented room? What about those who need a place to get away for a while—a young mother with three children under four, or someone who has lost his job? Who needs a chance to make friends? Who needs to relax? Who needs to laugh? When we invite people into our homes, we basically ask ourselves: "Who is there that we can serve?"

From the moment they walk through our door, our purpose should be to make them feel at ease. One woman I know conveys real joy at seeing me each time we meet. Her smile scatters sunshine, her arms are thrown wide to embrace me, and delight brightens her face. What an honor it is for me to be received in this manner. If we do nothing but make people feel we are glad to see them, we've gone far beyond this world's norm.

My pet peeve is groups where *no one* says a word of welcome. There is no excuse for this in the fellowship of the body of Christ. No business should supercede a smile that conveys, "So good to have you here." Refusing to give a greeting is for

190

many people the same as rejecting them. Their insecurities are so near the surface, their feelings of worthlessness so dominating, that we can give great healing if we do nothing more than say, "How glad I am to see you."

Conversation is one of the tools by which we put people at ease. Good conversation, for me, is very much considering the other person first. It is a matter of finding the right questions to ask that will discover their interests, their unique contributions to the world, their special areas of growth. Even in the purely intellectual pursuit of ideas, it is important to keep in mind that what this other person has to say is of merit. Even when we disagree, we must learn to be hospitable to his concepts.

One afternoon I invited a large group of women to come for coffee. We crowded around the dining room table and began to share common things from our daily lives. Somehow it seemed as though everyone was talking at once and no one was listening to the other person. I tipped my chair back, slipped into my mind's eye, and saw each person as a caricature of herself. Each one seemed to be saying only one word, "Me."

Over and over they repeated themselves, "Me. Me. Me. Me-me-me-me-me-me-me-me-me-me-me." Disgusted, I refrained from talking and contented myself with filling cups and passing cake.

However, the Lord had something significant for me to learn from that afternoon coffee klatch. He was soon asking, "Don't you do the same thing yourself? Isn't your conversation basically me-me-me? Aren't you mostly concerned about what people think of you, about expressing only *your* ideas, about having others think how cleverly you turn a phrase, how humorous your repartee is, what an eager mind you have, and how eloquent you wax?"

It was a moment of truth. Self-examination revealed that I entered a room personality-first, thought nothing of becoming the center of a party to the exclusion of others, dominated conversations, and fought inwardly to interject as many words

as possible into the discussion. I too needed to become a
"you-you-you" person. It has taken years, but I am learning to
say "you-you-you."

Good conversation is a matter of listening. When a Christian, filled with the Holy Spirit, listens, he listens on three
levels. He listens to what words are being said. He listens to
what the person really means by those words, and he listens to
the voice of the Spirit within who is giving illumination to his
hearing.

Often while sitting in conversations, certain phrases I've
heard take on sudden significance. What the talker meant by
his casual expression was deeper than he intended to convey.
The Spirit has given me knowledge totally apart from the
words which were just expressed. Unexpectedly I have come
to know some information about this personality; perhaps it is
a fear, or a problem, or the source of the problem. The next
step is to ask for spiritual wisdom as to what must be done with
this information. Am I to confront? Am I to keep quiet and
only pray? Am I to wait for more data in order to form a fuller
understanding? Am I to reach out in compassionate love?

This complicated capacity for listening deeply cannot be developed apart from learning to listen to the Lord in structured,
uninterrupted moments. In order to hear His voice we must
remove ourselves regularly from the busy, overly active, exciting, troublesome outside world. Contemplation, the fastening
of one's mind on one's Creator, is the only method by which
we can properly develop this interior silence and openness to
the spirit.

This lesson was pressed home to me by a godly woman who
once stayed in our home. "You know," she explained,"we
take all sorts of time talking to God, but we never take time to
listen to Him." Prayer is a neglected Christian discipline, but
the prayer of listening is the most neglected. We are familiar
with requests, less comfortable with thanksgiving, interces-
sion praise, confession, forgiveness; but we know next to

nothing about sitting before the Lord in quietness, waiting upon Him.

Each week, in addition to those other regular periods of prayer, I set aside several contemplation sessions. These may last from 15 minutes to an hour. Beginning always with praise, once I am aware of being in the Presence of the Lord, I start the process of disciplining my mind to listen. It is indeed a discipline. All the human realities begin to interject themselves. Dinners need to be prepared, phone calls made, writing planned—*No! It is You, Lord, I seek to hear, not these. Help me to fasten my mind on Your Presence.*

For many years I was tutored daily at His hand during these sessions. It was amazing how much there was to learn. After a while I began to experience silence. Sometimes there were infrequent directives as to ministry, and fewer awesome reminders from the Word as to needs for inner correction. But I began to learn that *the silence was in itself the voice of God.* This is the quiet of the Spirit, a communication which occurs without words.

I rose from these sessions of quiet bathed in a peace beyond understanding. It was not unusual that the moment I stood to my feet and opened my bedroom door, ministry began— someone called, tears choking the voice, or someone rang the doorbell needing to be encouraged. Because I had come so lately from that listening place, I was able to hear Him tell me what was needed for this person to be touched significantly. Learning to listen to God, giving Him the courtesy of unrushed communion, will automatically insure that quiet quality of being able to listen in a supernatural way to the needs of our fellowmen.

Phone courtesy is another area of hospitality which needs to be developed in our lives. This jangling device of human creation can be an absolute nuisance or a positive force for ministry, depending on the philosophy we choose to develop concerning it. Every pastor's family has probably had the feeling that their lives were being dominated, ruined, or controlled by insistent calls.

It is important to view the telephone not as a necessary evil, but as a means for facilitating ministry. How little have we Christians learned to use the discoveries of our technology as instruments for the good of the Kingdom.

The telephone, if used correctly, can facilitate ministry, build the communication within the Body, ease loneliness, bring comfort, provide a tool for giving cheer. It can be used in evangelism, counseling and contact work. Even prayers can be shared over the phone.

Since good manners are nothing more than making people feel at ease, they may mean working to convey warmth as we answer the phone for the umpteenth time. They may mean not giving up our bedroom if we sense this extra fussing is going to embarrass guests and they would really prefer sleeping on a cot.

For the Christian, good manners mean having the same hospitable spirit demonstrated by Christ—His openness, His eager reception of all humanity and their burdens. To aid us, we have the promise of His presence through the Holy Spirit. We have been inhabited by the hospitable Christ. Like Him, we can be hospitable in rooms without walls, in kitchens without counters. We each can develop the ability to put at ease all who come our way. This whole world is our home into which we can welcome God's creation.

In jostling crowds we can steady the arm of that elderly person for whom there is no concern. We can comfort that strange child in the store whose "mommy got lost." We can listen to the middle-aged woman who insists on talking during the entire train trip. We can reassure the stranger frightened about the wrong bus schedule. This created world is a vast hostel in which we can practice hospitality and courtesy and openness. It is indeed the world which God has made. Let us rejoice and be glad in it.

194

Life Response

1. Make a study of the Gospels to determine how often Christ asked questions in His conversations.

2. Test a week of your private conversations.

   a) How much of what you say is "me-me-me"? How much is "you-you-you"?

   b) Do you discuss the same topics over and over or are you able to participate in a variety of subjects?

   c) How much initiation in conversation is because of your efforts? Or do you wait until someone attempts to put you at ease?

   d) What is the basic topic of your talks? people? purchases and things you own or want to own? ideas and events? the realm of the spiritual?

3. Ask yourself how many levels of listening occur in your life. Are you listening at all, or only thinking of what you want to say next?

4. Set aside several times this week to listen to God. Place your notebook nearby and record in it what He says to you.

A Prayer

LORD,
THANK YOU FOR HAVING GIVEN YOURSELF in intimate,
inexplicable hospitality.
You have been the Host to all creation.

Without a dwelling, You have contained the
whole world and habited Yourself in the winds,
the corners, and the depths, inviting us to be
at home with You. Beneath the shadow of Your
wing You bid us hide, and in the depths of Your
Being You shelter and refuge us.

Without meat You have nourished us.
Without beverage You have refreshed us.
By Your very Word came sustenance.
On bread and water without price have we been fed.
You have been manna in the wilderness of our lives.

Without a table You have banqueted us,
inviting us, yea, to be married unto You.
Over our heads flies the banner of Your love.
We are entertained with the mysteries of faith,
the songs of the Spirit, holy laughter.
You have garmented us in festal righteousness.

As we wandered in wastelands,
You sought us before we called.
You extended eager welcome
though we had scarcely knocked.
You embraced us when we were filthy
and oppressed and undeserving.

You are the Samaritan who passes not by,
Who finds lodging for us in the warm inns by the way.
You bake fish over coals, waiting for us,
though we have forgotten to wait for You.
With broken hands You break the loaf of blessing.
Those same wounds caress our leprous spirits.
You do not fear to openly accept the intimate worship
of our harlot hearts.

You are the Host of all mankind.
Lifted up, suffering, without breath, You yet
extend greeting to all the masses,
        "Come unto me . . .
            come . . .
                come . . ."

You give us the mystery of Your presence
in this supper of the ages, this remembrance of
Your ultimate hospitality.

O Lord,
Make my hospitality as unto Yours.
Be forever my archetype of endeavor,
My firstfruit of harvested goodness:
Love for the battered, misused child,
Grace to bind running ulcers of flesh and soul,
Eagerness for the wealthy without servility,
And for the poor without superiority.

Through eternity You have been and will be
utterly hospitable.
Help me,
poor, faltering, unfeeling me,
to be like You,
with breath-beat and soul-heart
poured out
emptied
opened.
Help me,
to be given to hospitality.